The Art and Skill
of Managing People

The Art and Skill
of Managing People

W. H. Weiss

Parker Publishing Co., Inc.

West Nyack, New York

Library of Congress Cataloging in Publication Data

Weiss, W   H
    The art and skill of managing people.

    1. Personnel management. 2. Psychology, Industrial.
I. Title.
HF5549.W4312   658.3   75-5608
ISBN 0-13-048736-8

What This Book Will Do for You

"People are our greatest asset" is a statement made often by business executives when they discuss their companies. However, it falls to you, the individual manager, to capitalize on this asset, and to utilize it to the utmost of its capacity. It is, therefore, the art and skill that you, the manager, employ in handling these people that will ultimately decide how successful you will be as a manager.

THE ART AND SKILL OF MANAGING PEOPLE offers you the means of getting the most from those people whom you supervise, and upon whom your success rests. Application of the ideas contained in this book, which have been tested through years of practical experience, will help you to advance in your organization.

The problems that you face as a manager are not unique, although this knowledge does not make them any easier to cope with or to solve. As an experienced manager, I, too, faced these problems, and I searched desperately for some clue or guidance as to how I should handle them.

THE ART AND SKILL OF MANAGING PEOPLE deals with these problems and situations in a practical and realistic way. Chapter 4, for example, provides you with seven ways to be a better listener when dealing with your employees, and it also shows you how to make this skill pay off for you.

Not limited to how to handle your subordinates, I discuss the delicate and critical area of handling your boss. Chapter 7 not only explores the ways to get along with your boss, but it explains how you can become indispensable to him.

Another difficult situation you must inevitably face as a manager is disagreeing with one of your subordinates. Chapter 2 provides you with four ways to disagree firmly yet with sufficient tact so that you achieve the desired result along with the full cooperation of the employee. Also, this chapter gives you eight tested steps for selling an idea to your people in a way that will insure its acceptance.

I have included many case examples to illustrate how the art and skill of managing people really works. Typical of these case examples is the story of Oscar Boswell in Chapter 5. Oscar, the new operations manager of a 24-hour-a-day plant, inherited a tough situation. Planning was very poor and costs extremely high. Each morning Oscar met with his top three managers to review the previous 24 hours and plan for upcoming operations. The managers were told to make specific recommendations for cutting costs. This planning resulted in costs being cut over 40% in Oscar's first year, as well as a substantial monetary reward for Oscar.

Further dramatic examples are to be found:

- In Chapter 4 Gordon Leavy shows the value of giving effective instructions. After receiving new government regulations for environmental control, Gordon knew that the technical language would be very confusing for his people. He had the regulations rewritten and put into a form that was easy to understand. The company easily satisfied the government because of this, earning an award for the company and a promotion to vice-president for Gordon.

- A.T.&T's Customer Service Department increased morale and efficiency when the employees were allowed to sign their own names to customer replies. In Chapter 6 you will see how this small innovation led to larger ones that ultimately resulted in lower turnover, higher efficiency, and more satisfied stockholders..

- Chapter 8 provides an example of a manager who created enthusiasm among his people by making them proud of their work. To do this, C.L. Stover took the time to educate them about the volume, the customers, and the many uses of the company's finished products. Knowing this, the employees could point with pride to the important part that they had in creating those products.

Chapter after chapter is laced with key management tools, such as, ten ways to make your subordinates feel important, five rules for getting things done, and ten benefits of understanding your employees. Chapter 10 includes ideas on how to make your job easier, a subject of high priority.

THE ART AND SKILL OF MANAGING PEOPLE explains how you can reach your goals as a manager while at the same time helping your people to achieve theirs. Capable leaders are needed to handle today's management problems, and this book will aid you in becoming one of those leaders.

W.H. Weiss

Contents

6. How to Motivate Others to Work with You 103

7. How to Work with the Boss 125

The Art and Skill
of Managing People

1

How to Get Your People to Accept You

How to be Respected Rather Than Feared

It used to be that the boss was expected to be cold, unfriendly, and demanding. This was the way he supposedly got the respect of his people. But this type of leader never was respected and is not today. He is only feared. And with fear comes hate, since it's human to hate those you fear.

Nobody works willingly for someone he fears. When a subordinate respects his leader he plans and discusses problems with him; he goes along with what his leader wants him to do. He does not look for ways to betray or defeat him in his efforts.

Fear is built up when people do not know what to expect of their superior, when the superior is inconsistent and unpredictable. Nobody approaches a feared boss—why go "looking for trouble"? For instance, two supervisors are discussing a problem of scheduling which affects both of them. One speaks up, "Well, I suppose we ought to ask the boss to decide which job we should do first, but I sure hate to talk to him. If he's like he was yesterday, he'll chew me out for not knowing. I'd rather take the chance that we should run the large size first."

If a leader is tough one day and easygoing the next, he causes anxiety and uncertainty among the people he works with and those who work for him.

Robert A. Lull, president, Brooks International Corporation consulting firm, says, "People want to respect the company they're working for, they want to respect their boss, they want to think they're working for a company that's on the ball."

Avoid Domination

You can be respected rather than feared by keeping any feelings of superiority under your hat, by a friendly "we're working together on this" approach to people, and by putting away any thoughts of dominating others. People respect those who treat them as equals, who show no partiality, and who are fair and true in their actions.

People will look to you when you are respected. They will want your suggestions and advice. You, in turn, should show respect for your people.

An example of how a leader showed respect for a worker's feelings is the way in which supervisor Martin Weber talked to his millwright, Henry Jenkins: "Say, Hank, could you spare a few minutes to go with me to look at those new pumps you set yesterday? I'd like to talk over the problem you had with alignment. Maybe we can find a way to make the job easier."

A leader who gets things done through fear has no control when he is absent. One test of the respect for a leader is to see if progress is made when his people have jobs to do and he is not present to see that they are done.

The next time you are away from your job for a few days, get an insight into your status by noting how much was done while you were gone.

Respect Gains Help

The successful leader wins people to his point of view. As a leader, he needs to know *what* has to be done, as well as *how* it should be done. But he also needs the help of his subordinates to get things done. Respect gains him that help.

Some young or new leaders may think that they need to wear a sign "I Am the Boss" to be sure they get proper respect. They are mistaken. People are well-aware of whom they are working for and the status of individuals in a group. Leaders may limit their effectiveness by being aloof and staying away from their people.

Bill Baker, president, Chicago Sandblast, Inc., gets out on the job with his men. He's not afraid to do the dirty jobs or the distasteful ones. "I won't ask any of my men to do a job that I won't do myself. My men know this and they respect me for it. I feel my men do a better job than my competitor's men and that's why we've always got plenty of work to do," Bill explains.

Beware of Being Too Positive

One thing any leader must beware of is being too positive in his speech and actions. To be right as well as authoritative without adequate grounds is hard for subordinates to swallow, especially if it occurs day after day.

Ben Franklin had this problem until one of his friends called his attention to it. After that, Ben always prefaced his remarks and comments with "In my judgment . . ." or "I always thought that . . ." or similar words which seemed to suggest that he was not quite sure and was merely giving his opinion. He found that this approach made it easier for people to agree with him and go along with his desires.

If you sense someday that you may be getting too positive in your remarks and thereby turning people off, try Ben's philosophy and see if you aren't better accepted.

How to Gain Respect and Hold It

Sticking to your principles, even when those about you do not, will pay off in gaining respect. You will find also that you will have a higher opinion of yourself, and this will help to allay any doubts you might have of your ability to do a good job when you are put under stress.

Being firm and steady gains respect because it denotes a stability and control of one's emotions. You cannot always please everyone

—you accomplish nothing if you try to manage with this thought foremost in mind.

When a crisis arises in your department, do your people bypass you in favor of your boss or someone else when they should come to you? Maybe you need to improve their opinion of you to earn their respect.

Ten Ways to Earn Respect

Respect for a leader pays off in more efficient work along with a sense of camaraderie which makes cooperation enjoyable. Respect seldom comes automatically. You can earn the respect of your people by working for it. Here are ten ways you can achieve the benefits of respect:

1. Express appreciation for services performed. For instance, when someone does that little bit extra, something he didn't have to do, let him know that you appreciate his effort.

2. Be strong and consistent in the day-to-day performance of your job. A wishy-washy attitude one day, followed by a stubborn insistence on doing things your way the next, destroys people's confidence in you.

3. Keep an even disposition. Leaders have the right to become angry and upset, but not to show it. Temper tantrums are not in the repertoire of effective leaders.

4. Follow the rules. Leaders are expected to do things the right way and set examples for others. Rules are made for everybody, not just workers.

5. Avoid the obvious. People must be given credit for knowing the basic requirements of life. For example, nobody likes to be reminded to do something which he knows he must do and intends to do.

6. Shun foul talk, profanity, and obscene jokes. These are degrading and disrespectful. Leaders are expected to be above this type of talk. It's difficult for anybody to look up to someone whose language is uncouth.

7. Show respect for others and their viewpoints. They have a

right to their opinions, and they may be correct more often than you think. Giving respect gains respect.

8. Know your job and the boundaries of your authority. Nobody looks up to a leader if he is weak in his duties. Then again, overstepping your authority, especially when it's obvious, causes doubt and destroys your people's confidence in you.

9. Refrain from negative criticism. If somebody hears you negatively criticize someone else, he wonders how you talk about him to other people.

10. Admit your mistakes. Everybody makes mistakes. To not admit one shows weak character. Passing the buck says that you're unwilling to take the blame for your errors.

How to Learn of People's Interests and Needs

How do you learn of people's interests and needs? By talking with them, and, most important, by listening! Listening leads to understanding, and understanding people enables you to see what they like, why they have certain attitudes, and what they need. You can learn why they act as they do and be guided in your relations with them.

John Sisty, Chief, Engineering Division of the Veterans Administration Hospital in North Carolina, is a strong advocate of listening. He says, "If you want to motivate your men, listen to them. One of a manager's most important jobs is motivation, and you can't be a good motivator without being a good listener. Convince your people that you are interested in them personally. Nothing sets a man up in his job more than to realize that his boss is interested in him and recognizes him as a human being."

Too many times leaders pass off as unimportant the hobbies and the family life of their people. They fail to recognize the value of this information in getting along with the individual on the job. Common interests often exist and knowledge of them could lead to mutual respect. With respect comes understanding and cooperation.

Tomorrow, ask one of your people what he likes to do in his spare time. He will think more of you for your interest in him, and you will get a better insight into how he ticks.

Know What Your People Want

Do you know how your people feel about their jobs, what they want? You may have the opinion that their will to work isn't as strong as it should be.

Frank J. Schotters, director of personnel development at General Motors, says, "People don't want to take over the business. They still recognize their boss has to be a boss. But they want to participate, to be involved, to contribute the things they know. And they want what management wants—a better organization, more feeling of team spirit, and increased cooperation in doing a better job."

In the past few years a number of surveys have been made among workers in which they were asked what they want and expect from their jobs, and to rate the things in order of importance. Here are the findings of the surveys:

1. Appreciation and credit for work done
2. Being "in" on things
3. Interesting work
4. Fair treatment
5. Sympathetic help on personal problems
6. Understanding and patience
7. Job security
8. Good wages

The supervisors of these workers were also asked what they thought their workers wanted most. Surprisingly, the supervisors felt that good wages would be most important and job security would be second. It is apparent that workers generally rate the human part of their job as being more important than the monetary part.

These surveys illustrate that we can often be mistaken in what we think is important to someone else. It is necessary that you, as a leader, *know* what your people want, not what you *think* they want. Knowing leads to understanding, and there are many benefits from understanding your people.

Ten Benefits of Understanding

You can learn people's interests and needs by understanding them. Easy? No, but certainly well worth the effort. There are many benefits you can realize from knowing people's thoughts and feelings. Here are ten major ways that understanding pays off. Understanding:

1. Enables you to learn the reasons behind the actions of people.

2. Serves as a beginning point for presenting a proposal to someone.

3. Gives you insight into other people's viewpoint.

4. Makes you tolerant and forgiving of people's deeds.

5. Makes it easier for you to deal with those who are particularly critical, faultfinding, biased, and argumentative.

6. Gives you the ability to organize your thoughts in working with people and solving problems.

7. Helps you to recognize the rights of others.

8. Enables you to treat people as individuals and to recognize that each person is different.

9. Helps you to make decisions that are fair.

10. Makes you honest and true to others and yourself.

How to Use Pride in Handling People

By complimenting someone on something of which he is normally proud, you use pride to bring forth further good from him. To be successful in using pride, you must be sincere in your remarks. Also, what you compliment someone about must in *his* eyes be deserving of the compliment. If he does not feel it deserving, the compliment may backfire and be interpreted as ridicule.

An example of how an office manager might appeal to the pride of one of his clerks would be by approaching him and saying, seriously, "Hank, you have had a lot of experience with setting up filing systems, so I would like to get your advice on something."

In the maintenance shop the foreman uses pride as motivation by speaking sincerely to one of the mechanics, "You have done a nice job in reseating those valves, Bob, and I want to compliment you on it."

Complimenting someone on a particular task which he has done many times, each time the same way, does not ring true, and he will not feel deserving of a compliment. Look for the occasion when someone does a job unusually fast or under abnormal conditions. Your compliment will then be appreciated.

Jack Bessman, a mechanic, had been recently transferred into the maintenance department from his company's machine division where he had had the reputation of being a top-notch craftsman who was very adept with tools. His new supervisor, Bob Green, sensed that Bessman was a bit uneasy on the new job and needed to establish himself as a respected and skillful worker with his fellow men. Most of the work in the maintenance department was routine and simple in nature, work that any average mechanic could handle without difficulty, until the large compressor in Building 7 began using oil at twice its usual rate. Although Bessman had never seen this machine before, Green recognized the opportunity to provide Bessman a chance to demonstrate his skill.

As Green expected, Bessman soon had the machine again running normally. When Green complimented him for a job well-done, the supervisor knew that by the way the other fellows joined in, Bessman was now accepted and respected by his peers.

Pride Affects Emotions

The use of pride is a very strong tool in handling someone who is emotional. It has a calming effect in that it makes him feel important and worthwhile. The listener sees and realizes that he is understood, and he looks upon the one who gives compliments as a reasonable individual.

One of the differences between a good and an average teacher, especially when working with children, is how the good teacher gains the confidence and interest of the student. Pride in previous learning, brought out by the teacher, brings forth more effort in future learning.

Through appealing to someone's pride you can put him in a frame of mind to be especially receptive to a request you may make of him. His mood becomes agreeable and cooperative since you have demonstrated that your thinking is "right" when you complimented him.

How to Act as the One in Charge

Whether it's business, sports, or social activities, if you want to be looked upon as a leader, you must be able to act as one. How should you behave if you want to be considered as the one in charge?

You can tell who is the man in charge in a group or organization because he exhibits certain traits, skills, and abilities. Let's look at some examples of how the man in charge handles himself:

1. He is well-informed. He always seems to know the important details of recent incidents. His knowledge of the company, the department, and his job is very broad-based.

2. He understands people and knows how to communicate with them. He recognizes that he must speak his listener's language, and he will listen when spoken to.

Bennett Sack, vice-president of Copperweld Steel Co.'s Steel Bar Division, says, "Listen to your people—and not just to the key managers. There are many more people who can make a contribution. Talk to them. Tell them what you want from them, what you think they're capable of doing. And ask what you can do to help them. You'll never get results from the operation unless you tell people what you want."

3. He is almost always prepared. The man who goes to a meeting for which he has planned, organized, and prepared himself will be the one who runs the meeting, regardless of who actually called for it. The prepared man is able to take more responsibility and assume more power.

The man who is prepared easily adjusts to a new course of action. He's ready to redirect his interests, and makes a change without stress and strain.

Anyone with ambition and the desire to get ahead will find "being prepared" an easy step to his goal.

4. He doesn't expect to show up well in a popularity contest. The

path to effectiveness is by way of respect of subordinates, not their friendship. The man in charge is that because of his leadership qualities, not his social skills.

5. He shows a high level of honesty and courage. He indicates by his behavior that he understands those for whom he is responsible. He recognizes that his subordinates will make mistakes, and he is willing to let them do so in order to gain experience and acquire responsibility. As he strives to help others to grow and do better, he helps himself to do likewise.

Emotion and Reasoning

It is a well-known fact that decisions are based on much more than just logic and reason. All of us are influenced by emotion, and it plays a large part in our lives. We should learn how to handle it.

People think and act in two ways. They either reason things out or they decide through emotion. Reasoning involves dealing with logic and facts. Emotion concerns the feelings of people.

Most people consider themselves experts on logic and reason. They honestly believe that the statements they make and the acts they perform are logically and reasonably thought-out beforehand.

Yet studies have shown that 20 percent of their decisions are based on reason and 80 percent on emotion!

How to Contend with Emotion

It is a simple fact that if you are to get along well with others—if you are to influence their thinking—then you must be able to contend with emotion.

Dealing with emotion by reasoning is very difficult and many times just about impossible. Facts must prevail before decisions can be reached, and even then doubt may remain if strong emotion is present.

To overcome someone's emotion you must have his favorable attention. He must listen to you because he wants to, not because he has to. Any logic or reason you may have to offer means nothing unless you have worked at least this far with him.

How do you get someone's attention, his willingness to listen to you? He must know you and have a healthy regard for you. He must trust and respect you. Why else should he take the time to listen to you? These favorable opinions must be earned and they are not given easily.

You usually like the people who try to do and say things on your behalf. You listen to and respect someone who recognizes your importance by his awareness or actions. The man on the job has respect for the boss when the boss defends him and backs him in his actions.

Concede Before You Contend

The golden rule of dealing with emotion is to concede before you contend. In other words, *listen* before you talk. The other fellow has a right to his opinion. While you may not necessarily agree, there is always a *bare* possibility that he may be right.

You can say, "I didn't think about that," or "You have a point there." Take time to honestly consider his viewpoint. Put yourself in his position and see if you wouldn't feel as he does.

Before reasoning and logic can take over a discussion, emotion must be drained away. Give the other fellow a chance to get things off his chest, to blow off steam. He will feel better after he has done so.

When you approach someone in a delicate situation there are little things you can say which will show your respect for him. "Excuse me," "Please," and "Thank you" calm emotions and gain cooperation.

If you get in the habit of using these important words frequently you will find that you are better accepted.

Agreement

No two people always agree on everything. In a way, it is fortunate that people have different opinions, since this indicates that they think and reason in reaching conclusions.

Finding that someone does not agree with you should not bother you if you realize that it causes *you* to think and reconsider—actions which help you to understand others and improve yourself. You can still disagree agreeably and be calm and friendly while doing so.

Ted Farmer, production superintendent in a large steel mill, has a philosophy on agreement that works well for him. He calls it the "yes-but" technique. Of course, he is not the only one to find this way of agreeing, yet disagreeing, useful.

"Whenever I don't agree with the boss, I don't say 'No,' but I agree with his idea while at the same time offering him my opinion. I can say that he is right and I agree that something should be done or a procedure changed, but perhaps we can do it in another way.

"I proceed to explain my thinking. I'm sure the boss thinks more of me for not being a 'Yes' man all the time."

The "yes-but" technique is a good one for getting your ideas across. If you're not using it, why not give it a try tomorrow?

How Your Emotions Influence People

You influence people emotionally by your appearance, your actions, and your facial expressions. For example, a smile is important because it shows that you have a positive attitude and an optimistic viewpoint.

When you want to bring forth the importance of a situation, you can do so by being serious, solemn, deliberate, careful, concerned, determined, and dignified. When you want to promote a relaxed and pleasant mood you can do it by being calm, friendly, considerate, sympathetic, and cheerful.

What you say and how you say it carries an emotional connotation. Stuttering and stammering adversely affect presentations for they make the listener ill-at-ease, as well as distract from the subject matter. To some people these mannerisms suggest a lack of personal confidence in what is being said and an inadequate familiarity with the topic.

Poor grammar and word choice cause people to have a low opinion of the speaker. Continual blasphemy makes a poor impression for it suggests feelings of inferiority, lack of vocabulary, and inability to express oneself clearly on the part of the speaker.

How do people like Norman Vincent Peale and Billy Graham gain their following and acceptance? What makes them and others like them strong leaders? Part, if not most, of the answer lies in the emotional impact they have on their listeners.

Signs of Emotion

Aside from the common facial distortions, anger, crying, and laughing, emotion shows itself in other ways. For example, when we rationalize, we try to find reasons to explain why we acted as we did. In how we feel about other people, we look for a basis to accept the reasoning of someone we like, and a basis to justify disagreeing with the reasoning of someone we dislike. When we procrastinate, we find ways to delay making decisions when the outcome is feared or we are unwilling to take the responsibility.

You have a much better chance of getting your people to accept you if you can avoid the extremes of emotion. Displays of emotion embarrass some people and cause others to withdraw.

Inability to control emotions often leads someone to say and do things he later regrets. Take the case of the supervisor who was criticized by the manager of a machine shop for his high cost of tool replacement. The supervisor immediately blew his stack, saying to his men, "The next guy that breaks a tool will have to pay for it himself." Later that day, one of the most skillful machinists, who hadn't damaged a tool in his 20 years of service, accidentally stripped the threads on an expensive lathe. How do you suppose the supervisor got out of that situation?

How to Convince People You Are Fair

You are being fair when you make decisions on the basis of facts and conditions rather than on emotions. To be fair you must avoid being swayed by personalities and actions of individuals; you must think and act with facts as reasons.

You can show that you are fair if you refrain from showing favoritism, if you will listen to one man as much as to another, and if you are unbiased.

Studies by psychologists have revealed that people try to meet the expectations of leaders whom they know have high ethical standards. When working for an honest man it is difficult to be dishonest. If a man is fair to you, you tend to be fair to him.

How to Get Along with Almost Everybody

You can learn to get along with almost everybody if you recognize and remember that people are not alike. Since each person is different, each must be treated differently.

Many people feel that they know and understand others, but even the "people specialists," the psychologists, the psychiatrists, and the sociologists, have trouble understanding everyone. You would be very unusual if others' behavior never surprised you and if you knew everyone's feelings.

Getting along with everybody requires that you get along with yourself, that you recognize your own faults and weaknesses, and that you accept yourself for what you are. But, if you expect too much of yourself, then you probably expect too much of other people.

The "people specialists" believe that understanding yourself makes you more acceptable to others. Also, if you can believe people's expressed feelings about you, people will be more inclined to accept you. Your acceptance makes it easier for you to have people do what you want them to do.

2

How to Get People to Accept Your Ideas

What determines how well you and your ideas are accepted? If you know the answer to this question, you have an advantage because you then know what to say and do to realize acceptance. You should have little trouble in getting it.

While you may hope that your good feelings about people are accepted and returned, you may be disappointed to learn that this is not always true. Many people may be jealous of your accomplishments, and some may even feel that you have impeded their own. Others may look to you only as a way of getting ahead themselves.

You should be concerned about how people feel about you since your success in attaining your goals often depends on them.

You need people to accept your ideas. Here are some suggestions on what you can do to help yourself attain this end.

How to Say the Right Thing

The words you use are only part of how you communicate; your manner of using them is just as important. Emotions are involved, and emotions are usually stronger than reason. Your listener may not hear your words if your emotion is too strong.

Body motion, tone of voice, and facial expression often carry more weight than words. It pays to develop the proper mixture of words and emotion in your communications. The baseball team manager in protesting a call to the umpire makes his feelings well-known to the fans even though most of them cannot hear his words.

Being too positive in your statements can ruffle some people's feelings. You can avoid this by prefacing your remarks with, "It seems to me . . ." or "Isn't it true that . . . ?" Such an approach may help to win these people to your point of view.

Clint Jones, shop superintendent in the Acme Lumber Co. in Milwaukee, has the knack of getting the most out of the mill men without driving them or losing their respect, according to the president, Bruce Reeves. Bruce says, "Clint seems to know when to get tough and when not to. I've seen him talk pretty roughly to a fellow in the morning and joke with him in the afternoon. None of the men have complained to me about how they're treated, and our turnover is very low. I guess you could say that Clint knows how to say the right thing at the right time."

Avoid sarcasm if you wish your words to be kind. Sarcasm simply creates resentment—it doesn't help sell what you say. In the same vein, belittling results only in a loss of respect for the belittler and accomplishes nothing.

Your language is a factor in how you are accepted; many people use it as a measure of intelligence. Poor grammar, mispronounced words, and overuse of slang are indicators in some people's eyes of low standards. If your standards are not as high as people think they should be, your ideas may not be readily accepted. People feel they should be able to look up to their bosses and leaders.

How to Treat People

A leader's prestige among his subordinates is lowered when he acts differently in front of his superiors from the way he does when the superiors are not there. This false front is very apparent to the subordinates and often causes a loss of respect for the leader.

Be sure you treat your subordinates equally; showing favoritism is disliked. A wise supervisor spreads his jobs among his people so that all share in the easy and the hard tasks.

A domineering fellow may get his way if he's the boss, but he loses respect along the way. Acting the "big shot" and ignoring the "little fellow" make getting cooperation difficult. People may do as you *demand* if you are the boss, but they will not have their heart in their work. The result may be more errors and poor efficiency.

If you want to know how well-liked someone is, ask those who report to him rather than those to whom he reports. Today's young people in particular often try to learn how tough a boss is when considering whether to accept a job in his department. Their thinking is a carryover from their school days when they discussed their teachers before signing up for various courses.

You can increase your acceptability by displaying tolerance. Recognize that nobody is perfect, including yourself, and that everybody makes mistakes. People are different, so you can expect them to think and act differently. A feeling of respect for the opinions of the people you work with will bring about a greater exchange of ideas and better thinking.

Clayton V. Adams, supervisor for the Milne Construction Co., Portland, has learned that he should treat his men as equals when discussing problems. He has found that the men will be more cooperative if the atmosphere is informal and if everybody participates in working out problems.

The next time you are faced with a problem requiring creativity or thought, ask some of your people for help. "How would you do this, Joe? I'm stumped," or "What do you suggest, Bill?" are good approaches to make your people feel worthwhile and capable on the job. People like to be asked their opinion—it makes them feel important.

How to Promote Yourself

What we think of ourselves is often evident to other people. While a certain degree of ego is necessary for well-being, the self-satisfied man is not always well-liked. Yet, to get ahead you must occasionally call attention to your accomplishments. You can do this without offending others by talking to those people who can help you get noticed, such as your superiors. Of course, there are other ways to promote yourself, too. For example, you can write for publications and you can participate in various activities which will bring your name before the public.

Sincerity and honesty are the virtues of the accepted individual. What do you say when you are asked a question you can't answer? Admitting that you just don't know is almost always the best policy. Nobody is an expert on every subject. The man who always professes to know the facts must be suspect. Sooner or later, people will discount much of what he says.

Take the truth seriously. If you are honest and fair, people will soon learn to trust you. Watch how you handle promises. If you ever find that you can't do something in the time you promised to, by all means explain why. If you are silent you give the impression of not caring.

The enthusiastic and optimistic fellow is welcome in most groups because his type is usually efficient and gets things done. He brightens up the situation, relieves tension, and gets people to cooperate. A party host labels him as a "good mixer" and welcomes his presence.

A confident individual can inspire others, and so can the enthusiastic one. If you think positively and try to be optimistic much of the time, you will find more of your ideas being accepted.

How to Speak the Listener's Language

Your success in getting your ideas accepted may depend on the language you use. How do you handle the problem of not talking up nor talking down to people?

The answer is to use the language of your listener. By speaking his language you will be using words with which he is familiar. This means there will be less chance of mistakes.

Too many of us talk and write over the heads of others. Most of the time we are unaware that we are not being understood. By watching our language we could do a better job of communicating. For example, we often are guilty of using jargon.

Jargon is the name for verbal fuzziness of various sorts, such as wordiness and the use of abstract words that add nothing to the meaning of a statement. It is also the talk of the man who is so wrapped up in his job or hobby that only another person of the same profession knows what he is talking about. Bankers and lawyers in particular have this problem.

Why Do People Use Jargon?

There are several reasons why jargon gets into our language. First, someone may become so accustomed to the "language" of his profession that he simply forgets that not all people use and understand his words. Unless he tries to use the terminology of the layman and watch his listeners for indications of their understanding, he will probably fail in his efforts to communicate.

Second, a user of jargon may be only trying to impress others with his knowledge or experience. He's the amateur acting like a professional. For example, he may have heard scientists discussing a theory and now uses some of their terminology. Thus, he is trying to imply that he's an authority on space travel by using the words of the experts in this field. (Or, perhaps he will use specific words to mislead his boss about his knowledge of a particular subject.)

Third, the user feels that "talking jargon" gains acceptance and cooperation. If you want to be accepted by a special group, must you not speak the group's language? A supervisor may use the worker's slang in hopes of being considered "one of the boys." An accountant may use engineering terms in asking for help from an engineer on a cost problem.

Fourth, jargon may be used to cover up one's lack of something important or meaningful to say. Too, the jargon user may be trying to present that which he has to say in a way which makes it difficult for others to disagree with him. He does this by making his meanings and intentions unclear. A consultant might try to avoid being clearly understood in order that his client will continue to retain his services. A writer may be unable to reason logically or to present interesting material; he may use pretentious language to conceal these facts.

Fifth, using jargon is a way of avoiding direct statements. The politician likes jargon because he can give stock comments on issues to gain a desired effect with a minimum of intellectual effort and without committing himself to a definite program. An engineer might use it to explain a design difficulty to management when he isn't quite sure of himself or hopes to cover up his inability to cope with the problem.

Jargon's Pitfall

Using jargon makes us become lazy communicators. It can almost do your thinking for you once you learn it. Look how easy it is to start your letters by saying, "We appreciate your apprising us of this matter and certainly will give it due consideration," or "You are advised that . . ." or "As a matter of concern, we shall be interested in knowing . . ." Such writing is cold and stiff. The reader may feel a lack of true concern on the part of the writer.

Amos Greene, the manager of the Customer Relations Department of a mail order company in California, found that the company frequently received multiple letters from customers concerning product complaints, payment of bills, and delivery delays. He realized that this indicated customer dissatisfaction and that the company's reputation for fair dealing was at stake. After investigating specific cases, Amos learned that many of the letters were written simply because the customers felt they weren't being treated with respect, the company wasn't really "trying" to correct matters.

His solution to the problem was to begin a training program for his people on writing of letters and handling of customer problems. The instruction stressed showing more concern on the part of the company, better explanations of difficulties, use of simpler and more understandable words, and making the communication more personal and sympathetic.

The training program accomplished its objective—fewer second and third letters were received from customers. As an added benefit from the program, employees in other departments also began to see that fewer mistakes were made in filling orders and that deliveries were made more promptly.

How to Avoid Jargon

How do you avoid jargon in your talking and writing? How should you communicate to be more easily understood?

You can express yourself as simply as possible. You can try to let facts speak for themselves instead of giving them more emotion and drama than they deserve. You can stay away from clever and cute expressions; you can eliminate words which have fancy or smart connotations.

You can cut unnecessary words. Simple words and sentence structures are easier to understand and far more effective. You can forget about trying to impress others when all you intend to do is inform them.

This is not to say that your communications should be stilted and cold. The conditions and situations under which you communicate should be considered. Circumstances should determine the tone and style of words you use. Is the setting formal or informal? Will simple words or slightly uncommon words be most appropriate? It is equally bad to say "it ain't so" among English professors as it is to say "that is a prevarication" among high school students. In the first case you will be accused of talking like an uneducated person, and in the second, of talking like a professor. Unusual words may express your message more accurately but may not be in good taste. Also, you should not use difficult words only to display your mastery of such words.

Another problem must be considered. Is the listener receptive to what is being said? Does he place the same meaning on the words as the speaker? Preconceived opinions of what a listener expects to hear may cause him to hear just that, and to ignore and disregard anything to the contrary. There is always a doubt when highly technical words are being used that the one receiving the message really understands. The following story is an illustration of this:

Hoping that the Internal Revenue Bureau could be persuaded to extend the deadline for payment of his income tax, a taxpayer sent the Bureau a letter asking for a month of grace. The answer he received read as follows:

"The Internal Revenue Bureau does not assume a panegyrical, eulogistic, or encomiastic viewpoint toward the delay of remittance of tax due the government."

The taxpayer sensed permission and wishing to thank the Bureau he wrote back:

"I am pleased to learn that it is OK for me to pay my tax a month late. Thank you."

The Bureau realized that there was a misunderstanding so immediately wrote a second letter:

"The postponement of tax payment is an interdictive action and
will be abnegated by the government authority."

The taxpayer acknowledged the second letter:

"Thank you again for allowing me another month. It will save me
some money."

A third letter was sent by the Bureau:

"You must pay by April 15. We'll fine you if you don't!"

The taxpayer finally got the point, but only after some needless
correspondence.

There's a Place for It

Jargon, nevertheless, does have its place. Actors put across their
part by using expressions typical of the people they're portraying. The
Englishman drops a few "bloody's" here and there and the Southerner
must come out with "you-all" now and then. Writers have their charac-
ters talk true to life. Every specialist uses a language of his own. And
why shouldn't professional people in *conferring with one another* use
their technical language? There may actually be less chance of being
misunderstood if they do.

It pays to learn the other man's language, if only to a slight extent. You can understand what he's talking about. When he realizes
this, he's going to be more willing to cooperate and help you with your
problems.

There's proof that jargon is going to be here for a while. A
government agency in referring to its use has this to say: "Much of the
work of the Revenue Service depends on the use of legal and technical
terms; we are obliged to phrase our letters in such a way that there are no
loopholes for possible misinterpretation."

The writer hastens to add, however: "We have no choice in this
matter of legal language—we have to live with it. There is, however, no
rule that says we are forbidden to add translations of passages into
language taxpayers can understand."

How to Sell Your Idea

If you have a good idea you naturally want to let people know about
it. You want to be given recognition; you'd like to have your company

gain the benefits. But before you can realize these things you need to do a selling job.

Some people hesitate when it comes to promoting themselves or their ideas. For one thing, they may fear being turned down. For another, they may feel that the benefit is not worth the effort of selling it. They may be discouraged with the amount of work necessary to put an idea across.

Your idea may be just what the boss ordered and the answer to the company's problem, but unless you can get acceptance, it's not worth much to anybody. How can you sell your idea, make sure your boss or your people understand it?

You need to follow a planned course of action. Here is the way to go about it.

Eight Steps to Selling an Idea

1. Be enthusiastic. If you are not convinced that your idea is good, how can you expect to convince other people?

2. Give reasons why you are behind your idea and what conditions or history prompted your study. Know all the pros and cons. Do a thorough job of investigation before you start your sales approach.

3. Be clear and specific in your presentation. Show your listener *how* he can gain instead of just telling him he will. Give concrete examples in terms that anyone can easily see and accept. Instead of saying that much time will be saved, say *how much* each day or month. Point out specific advantages of your idea rather than simply saying it has many.

4. Explain the order of events. Show *what* has to be done first. Tell what will occur after this is done. Make your explanation logical and to the point. Omit minor details which might confuse your listener.

5. Explain *why* your idea will work and why in a certain way. People become more interested and willing to cooperate when they can see reasons for actions. They also want to be *in* on things. Understanding helps them in this respect.

6. Try different means of communicating. Some people better

understand what they read, others what they hear. Give a bit of each, appealing to the sense your listener prefers. Simple examples help to sell complex ideas.

7. Make your idea more attractive by pointing out its monetary worth. Savings over what is now being spent goes over strong with those who will decide the worth of your idea. The monetary appeal may be the most important part of your selling argument.

8. Summarize your sales talk with the high points of your presentation. Follow up with an organized report if your proposal is complex or lengthy.

How to Disagree Pleasantly

While it's better to be agreeable in order to get along with everybody, sometimes you find that you must disagree with someone. In handling people, your skill in disagreeing determines how successful you are in persuading and in getting people to accept your ideas.

When you must disagree, you certainly want to be tactful and avoid causing hard feelings. You want to make it as easy as possible for the other fellow to come over to your side without embarrassment or loss of face.

The way to disagree pleasantly is to relax and smile while you express your feeling. Being too serious causes your listener to tighten up, increase his resistance, and even build up resentment.

An important point in disagreeing is not to be too objective. If you try to base your disagreement solely on facts without your own thinking and feeling as reasons, your listener may simply dig up facts and figures to the contrary.

Bob Rupert, head of the Rupert Associates agency, attests to the problem of using only facts to persuade people. "I have to be darn sure of my facts when I disagree with one of my department managers because this fellow is well-read and has a remarkable memory. He has the ability to come up with some statistic which is contrary to one I may have mentioned, for example, on market research. In our business many of these things are pretty intangible anyway."

David B. Albright, president, Akron Savings & Loan Company,

Akron, Ohio, frequently speaks on the art of disagreeing. In one of his talks he mentioned a businessman he knew who was an expert at this skill. This fellow's technique was saying, "Doggone it, you're usually right, probably this time, too; but could I talk you into going out on a limb with me just this once?" Usually the other fellow went along with this approach.

Four Ways to Disagree Tactfully

The ability to disagree tactfully can be of tremendous value in handling people, both in social and business relations. Many times you will be faced with a situation in which you cannot agree with someone, yet do not wish to risk offending him. That someone could be a close friend, a customer, a fellow worker, or the boss. Being able to express an opposite viewpoint *tactfully* may enable you to convince the other fellow that you are right, avoid mistakes, and get more done without irritating him. How is it done? Here are four ways to disagree tactfully:

1. Talk about facts. Avoid saying you disagree. For example, say "our records show that we make most of our sales in the spring," or "accounting figures show that we need at least a 10 percent mark-up over factory cost if we are to break even." You might also quote the statements of people who should know and who are respected. Another way is to refer to a newspaper story or publication which backs up your viewpoint.

2. Suggest alternatives. Rather than flatly opposing what someone has advocated, offer other ways in which the problem may be solved or the goal reached. Mentioning alternatives gives the other fellow a choice, causes him to think more, yet still leaves the decision of the best course of action up to him.

3. Praise but redirect. Maybe you can't agree that someone's answer to a specific problem will work, but why not verbally look for the worth of it for solving some other problem? Such a comment certainly prevents the sting of a refusal or an outright objection while still acknowledging that the individual is trying and is capable of coming up with a better answer.

4. Ask for further help. While you may disagree, it will not be

necessary for you to say so if you instead ask for additional ways of taking action. When you ask for someone's help, you indicate that you respect him. You also suggest to him that he has the skill and knowledge to be of aid to you.

How Disagreeing Can Gain Respect

It takes very little in many cases to get someone to change his opinion and agree with you. You probably know someone who has a positive way of stating things. If no one raises a question, his opinion is outwardly accepted and he has his way. But often this fellow is simply testing his opinions against others. If an opposite viewpoint is expressed or facts are presented to dispute him, he is often willing to yield. With his yielding he also concedes a certain amount of respect to the one disagreeing with him.

Beverly Bond, office supervisor of the Thompson Corporation, noticed that the other supervisors in her department seldom, if ever, disagreed with Joe Black, the office manager. She knew that they felt he was sometimes wrong from remarks they made away from the office. Beverly had strong convictions about some matters backed by experience with another employer. She found that she could disagree with Joe and often convince him of her way of thinking. But more important, he occasionally asked her advice, something he didn't do with the other supervisors. She had gained his respect by not always agreeing with him.

When you feel strongly that your superior may be wrong, and especially when you have facts to back your opinion, by all means let him know your feelings. Being proved right will gain you respect.

How to Say "No"

Leaders are forever being asked for something. If you have people working for you, you also will have that problem. You will be asked for favors, permission, advice, and a raise in pay. Unfortunately, you cannot always grant these things. Although you may feel that you would be better accepted if you could respond favorably more often, many times the proper and only answer is "No."

But there isn't any reason why you shouldn't try to soften the blow of the "No" when you give it. You can learn to say "No" almost as pleasantly as saying "Yes." Put yourself in the other fellow's place by asking yourself, "How, in a similar situation, would I like to be treated?"

Dr. Gene Dalaba, corporate and regional manager of behavioral systems at Towers, Perrin, Forster, & Crosby, Inc., San Francisco, says, "Never let a man walk away from you with your 'No' answer unless he is aware of exactly why you felt you had to say 'No'."

The cold, impersonal "No" which leaves no room for doubt should be avoided at all costs. Examples of such negative responses are a form letter refusal to a request, the "sold out" sign at a store, and the insincere voice on the telephone saying only "sorry" followed immediately by the line being disconnected.

Michael Caparon, communications manager, Packaging Dept., Dow Chemical Co., feels strongly about the impersonal "No." He says, "I try never to say 'No' unless I leave a way out for a man. There is usually some component of his request or proposition that has merit. Why trample a man with a flat 'No'? As I say, leave him some dignity—some way out."

Even a personal "No" can be harsh. The way to best handle a refusal is to give it with honesty and understanding, using the most kind words you can.

When "No" Is Not the Answer

There are times when a leader must be careful not to say "No." An employee who has been doing a great deal more than has been asked of him and who needs a rare special consideration is not really asking for a favor. In a way he is entitled to be treated just as well as he has been treating his company.

Ray Wilson, factory clerk, worked several evenings near the end of the month without pay in order to bring the preventive maintenance records up-to-date. Later in the week when he asked his boss, "Robby" Robins, for a few hours off in the afternoon to take his child to the zoo, "Robby" replied, "Sure, Ray, you have earned it. I appreciate your staying over those evenings to work on the records. The men won't be doing any unnecessary work now since we're up-to-date.''

How to Overcome Objection to Detail

When people have accepted your proposal in principle but bring up reasons for turning down the idea which are not part of the idea itself, you must find ways to overcome these objections to detail. For instance, your superior may agree that several of the file cases in the office should be moved to a storage area so that more working space will be available. But this will require that the clerks spend quite a few hours rearranging the files and discarding some of the papers. Your superior feels that the clerks are too busy to spend any time doing this.

The first step in overcoming objection to detail is to acknowledge the problem—in this case, the clerks not having time to work with the files. This shows your superior that he is right in pointing out that your idea cannot be easily carried out.

Then eliminate or minimize the objection by suggesting something that *you* can do to overcome it. Maybe you can offer the help of some of your people. If this is not possible, suggest something your superior can do to reduce the objection.

To counter objections to detail, you should also point out the strong benefits of your idea, both to your superior and other people. Get others to support you. Try to show how the advantages of following your proposal provide benefits *well-worth the efforts* necessary to get it done. In the case of the files, for example, you can mention the greater efficiency and safety which result from more working room, and how appearance of the office will be improved.

The office manager of a Detroit insurance company, George Lindholm, found that often when he suggested to Tony Stingo, a section manager, that a change be made in an office procedure, Tony went along with the idea but soon afterwards would object to some minor detail. The manager then had to spend time finding a remedy to overcome the objection. As a result, the beneficial impact of the change was diminished and doubt was raised as to whether or not the change was really desirable.

Determined to avoid these objections, George made sure that he foresaw any possible problems the next time that a change in procedure seemed advisable. He also began asking Tony for his opinion and to help with the handling of details if the change were to be adopted. After that, George no longer had any problems getting his ideas accepted.

3

How to Get Other People
to Agree with You

There are several ways you can get people to agree with you. It is best, of course, if people willingly want to go along with you rather than do so because they think they must to hold their jobs or maintain their status.

Getting people to agree with you is easier if they respect you, if they look up to you as a leader. You can promote this image by being skilled in how you approach people, by being knowledgeable in what you say and do, and by pointing out how much people can gain by agreeing with you.

How to Approach People

Approaching people with the viewpoint that they are important and that their opinions are respected brings out the best in them. You need to get to know your people in order to do this.

A good way to start knowing more about your people is to spend time with them. For instance, you might try occasionally sitting down in the lunchroom with them. If it seems a little awkward to do this by yourself, pick out someone you know fairly well and invite yourself to go with him when he joins his fellow workers. You can use a pretense of wanting to discuss a common interest (other than one from the job), and after you've talked about it a bit, bring other people into the conversation on other subjects.

Another way to learn about your people and make them feel important is to notice when someone is off the job and comment about it when he returns. Saying that you missed him and hope that nothing serious caused his absence will prompt him to talk, giving you the opportunity to learn about him and his family.

According to Wilbur A. Erskine, Assistant Treasurer of the Cambridge, Massachusetts Gas Co., "The supervisor who has an honest concern for the well-being of his people will gain their respect and good will. He should take a sincere interest in their personal lives and do whatever he can to help them with their problems. This will give them a feeling of kinship with the boss that will show in good work performance."

Approach Affects Productivity

What your people believe you think of them often is a factor in their productivity. Jack Hall, engineering manager, sensed that he was not getting all the cooperation he should from his maintenance people. They appeared to slow down, even to stop working, when he observed them on his trips through the plant. Jack mentioned this to his supervisor, Bill Henry, when they talked about improving the productivity of the group.

Bill told Jack that the manager was right in his observation. Some of the maintenance men had told Bill that they had noticed "the big boss was 'checking-up' on us again today," and they didn't like this. Bill suggested that Jack refrain from watching the men work, particularly from a distance.

The engineering manager took his supervisor's advice. After that, when he went out into the plant to inspect equipment or study troublesome operations, he made a point of coming up to the men to talk about the equipment and to agree with them whenever he could on how they were handling the repair. He looked for opportunities to praise their skill on the job and on previous work which they had done. His approach of talking with his people rather than merely observing them changed their thinking that he was critical of their methods or their productivity.

How to Get People to Think

People who can get things done are invaluable to an organization. Such people usually have developed their ability to think and reason. They use this skill to motivate people.

Studies have shown that the need for ability to handle human relations is much greater than the need for technical skill in today's managers; skill in human relations requires thinking about how to act, what to say, and what to do to handle people's problems.

Peter Lindsay, the director of a large marketing business, found that his department managers were unable to offer practical solutions and suggestions to problems he brought up at his monthly meeting. He wanted more from his managers and was determined to get it without having to ask a second time.

To handle the problem, Peter began sending out a memo to each manager a few days prior to the meeting; the memo briefly stated the problems and requested that they be prepared to offer their suggested solutions and recommendations. This enabled the managers to investigate and think about the problems before they came to the meeting. The result was more extensive participation and quicker response on the part of the managers, both of which helped the organization.

People often need to be pushed to think. Most of us use only a small part of our capability to solve problems, find better ways to do our work, and improve ourselves. A leader should be an example to his people in showing them how to better themselves through using their mental abilities. Some of the ways he can do this are by being methodical in his approach to problems, showing creativity, and being cautious in reaching conclusions.

Kenneth J. Conn, dispatcher with Tucson, Arizona Transit Corporation, tries to get his people to think about their work. He says, "If a man is having some problem out on the route, I give him my full attention when he talks about it. By asking him what he thinks of two or three possible solutions to the problem, I can usually get him to figure out for himself which is the best of several ways to handle things."

The next time one of your people comes to you with a problem, take the time to say, "Let's think this thing out a bit," and then *do* just that. You'll find that you'll feel better, and so will he, about how you decided to proceed than if you simply had jumped to the first answer that came to mind.

How to Handle Promises

Anyone who fails to keep a promise disappoints others. Also, if that person has any conscience, he suffers a guilt feeling himself. To make matters worse, the one who is disappointed becomes irritated if the failure to keep a promise is repeated.

How should you handle promises? What should you do to help yourself to keep those you make? Here are a few things you can do to stay out of trouble with promises:

1. Don't promise something just to relieve an immediate pressure or only to please someone.

2. Keep a record or make a mental note of your promises to help you remember them. Also, carry out promises at your earliest opportunity.

3. Look upon a promise as a personal commitment of your word, a serious obligation which reflects on your sincerity and honesty.

Making promises puts you on the spot—you must deliver. If you can promise to *do your best* in working towards an objective rather than positively assure an action, you lighten the load for the situation when you are unable to completely fulfill what you intended to do.

There's a danger in promises. Mark Twain said, "To promise not to do a thing is the surest way in the world to make a body want to go out and do that very thing." Of course, Mark Twain said this in jest. But a promise may curtail an action you'd like to take and prey on your mind. *Be careful what you promise.*

How Accuracy Helps to Get Agreement

Being accurate causes you to be remembered, and a continual pattern of accuracy soon will earn you a desirable reputation. Contrast this to the way people feel about someone who frequently guesses—the guesser soon finds that people no longer bother to consult him because they don't know whether he is guessing or really knows the answer to a question.

Bluffing seldom works out well, either because, sooner or later, facts come to light which make the bluffer look bad. Similarly, broad-sweeping statements and exaggerations, if frequently offered, take away someone's credence and lead to distrust. It's much better to admit that you do not know something rather than be proved wrong later. If you must guess occasionally by being pushed to do so, guess on the under rather than over side—you'll look better as well as let the other fellow have his fun later when he gives you the facts.

Being accurate helps your company in dealing with other companies and in keeping its customers. The billing and accounting people in an organization must keep their errors to a minimum to maintain the company's image of being honest and reputable.

June Hostutler, billing clerk for a large drug company, says that she always double-checks an invoice for the quantity and the price before she sends it out. She knows that their customers will confirm these items before paying and immediately question any figures that do not appear correctly. People can and do feel that if a company is careless in its billing, it may also be careless in the quality of its products.

If you are involved with determining or approving the pay of the individuals who work for you, take particular care to be accurate. People expect their employer to pay them what they are due—they are unhappy and quite critical when errors are made, especially when they are to the company's advantage.

Get the reputation for being accurate. It will help when you are quoting facts and figures in an effort to get people to agree with you on a decision.

How to Accept Complaints

You cannot please everyone all of the time so you may as well accept the fact that there will always be someone who is unhappy with what you've said or done. Invariably someone will tell you that he does not agree with you. If you work with him it is better that he lets you know why he disagrees so that you will know what is bothering him and be able to explain or answer his complaint.

The most important thing for you to do when someone complains is to listen carefully and hear him out completely before you attempt to answer. By so doing you show that you are truly concerned and want to hear the entire story. By being quiet and letting someone "unload," you make the complainer feel better. Sometimes all he may want is someone to listen to him—he may already accept the fact that nothing can be done to change what he is unhappy about.

In addition to doing a good job of listening, you should accept complaints or criticism gracefully and with a cooperative attitude. Here are some ways to do that:

1. Avoid finding fault with someone who is complaining. Do not give the impression that he does not know what he is talking about, or that he has some motive for complaining other than the issue itself.

2. Be serious and concerned. This is no laughing matter to the complainer. He will not be pleased if you joke or make fun of him, especially if he already has felt hurt.

3. Don't make the complaint worse than it really is because this suggests you reverse roles with the one who is complaining. For instance, don't originate a complaint of your own by exaggerating so that the complainer must go on the defensive.

4. Stay on the subject. Don't try to avoid the issue by talking about something else. If anything, explore the problem with the other fellow so that you make it clear to him that you want to fully understand his complaint.

5. Accept the criticism with broad shoulders. Don't give the impression that you are personally hurt by the complaint and that any remedy would seriously tax you.

The Pennsylvania Mutual Life Insurance Company suggests to its employees that they never argue with the public. Instead, a complaint or criticism should be replied to with words such as "I may be wrong; I sometimes am. Let's examine the facts together," said pleasantly. Such an approach to a delicate situation often pays off in keeping customers happy and at the same time retaining their goodwill.

How to Get Cooperation

There is no easy way to get cooperation. Don't think that there are some special words to say or ways to act that will always cause people to jump at the opportunity to help you.

A newly-appointed manager may be surprised to find that his subordinates aren't as cooperative as he thought they would be: some of the work he delegates doesn't get done in the manner he expected, and some doesn't get done at all. This bothers him until he finally realizes that all people are not as conscientious and willing to cooperate as he is. If he has not already been aware of it, he now sees one of the reasons for his promotion.

The best way to get cooperation is to recognize that people are human, not perfect, and they have faults, just as you do. Try to see their viewpoint and how they feel when they are asked to do something. Listen to what they say about the job, how they think it should be done, and then go along with as many of their suggestions as you can.

People want to be able to decide how they do their job and a voice in decisions affecting them personally. They want interesting work, not simple, repetitive chores. If they can get this on their job, they're more willing to cooperate.

Frederick Hersberg, professor of management at the University of Utah, has a theory about the problem of maintaining employees' interest in their job. He thinks that there has been a decrease in the will to labor, but not in the will to work. Hersberg feels that workers look for something to do that goes beyond a mere fulfillment of duty.

Robert Townsend, former chairman of Avis Corp., urges management to give employees a significant hand in making business decisions. He says the problem of managers is that they insulate themselves from the problems of the plant and the assembly line. Managers should get to know their employees on a first-name basis, and workers should be encouraged to learn more than just one job.

The man who gets cooperation usually has given something first in that he has shown interest, respect, and enthusiasm towards the job and the people involved.

How to Improve People's Faith in You

Be consistent if you wish to have people have faith in you. The thing that worries your workers is how you will react to them. If they know what to expect from you, they will be more at ease. Everybody gets along better with the boss who has an even temperament.

Your workers need to know that a good job done one day will get your recognition the same as when done another day. They want to receive your favorable attention every day, not just on the days you are feeling good.

People are more willing to accept others and cooperate if they feel important. When they think they are important, they also feel obligated to give more of themselves.

Ten Ways to Make People Feel Important

When you make someone feel important he looks upon you as a reasonable, perceptive individual, one that recognizes his worth and is willing to promote his welfare. Making someone feel important gains his willingness to agree with and work for you.

Here are ten ways to make the other fellow feel he is "special."

1. Ask his advice. Although you may feel that you have more and better information or knowledge than he could contribute, you may be surprised by what he has experienced and can offer. Asking his advice implies that you think his opinion is worth considering.

2. Remember his name and use it frequently when talking with him. The most important word to an individual is his name. Of course, you must be sure that you pronounce it correctly, and even asking this of him makes him feel important.

Franklin D. Roosevelt always repeated a stranger's name three times in the first few minutes of conversation with him so that he could remember it more easily. Conrad Hilton insisted that every employee of his hotels who learned a guest's name use it in addressing him. These men recognized the value of knowing someone's name and using it.

3. Discuss subjects but never argue about them. When you argue you are saying that the other fellow is wrong, even though you may not use that word. If you insinuate he is wrong, how can he feel important?

4. Sincerely compliment him occasionally. There is something to praise about everyone. A compliment says that you think what someone is doing or did is deserving of attention and to be commended.

5. Be more willing to listen than to talk. Pay close attention and show interest when he talks to you. Your willingness to take the time to do this tells the other fellow you respect him.

6. Direct the conversation to his accomplishments and his interests rather than your own. Everybody enjoys talking about himself and letting the world know what he has done. The fact that you should ask about his deeds proves their importance.

7. Be interested in him. Ask if there is anything you can do for him. Keep him well-informed on all matters which may concern him. Why else would you do this if he were not important?

8. Give him opportunities to do things he usually isn't privileged to do. Provide him with benefits other than he usually gets for job accomplishment. Give him a chance to perform unusually well so that he will look good in the eyes of others.

9. Show respect for his knowledge and wisdom by repeating a remark of his. You show that you were impressed with something he said when you are able to repeat his words, as he said them, sometime later.

10. Treat him with courtesy, dignity, and respect. This can "puff him up," especially if he feels inferior. He may not often experience this treatment and therefore particularly appreciate it.

Plant Manager A. D. Putnam was aware that his laboratory manager had an inferiority complex. When Howard Stone had been promoted to the position from Chief Chemist, he had accepted it almost apologetically, saying that he wasn't sure he could handle the job. Putnam believed that if he could make Stone feel more important, he would do a better job of managing the technical people. A visit from the company vice-president in charge of research gave Putnam the opportunity to do this.

Putnam took the vice-president to the lab and introduced him to Stone. In his presence, he told the vice-president what Stone had accomplished with his people and how important their efforts were to the company's growth and future operations. From that day on, Putnam never again needed to be concerned about the initiative and aggressiveness of his laboratory manager.

A long distance truck driver passing through a small town on his trip was halted by a stoplight in the middle of the town. As he waited, an unhappy-looking girl crossed the street in front of him. He opened the window of his cab, leaned out of the window, and greeted the girl with, "Hi! I hope that you have a nice day." The girl turned and smiled at this unexpected friendliness. When the driver resumed his trip, his co-driver turned to him and remarked, "You must be out of your mind. What did you do that for?" The driver answered, "Buddy, I was just making her day a good one. It makes her feel good, and it makes me feel good, too."

How to Be Noticed

We all like to be noticed, especially when it leads to a pat on the back or a compliment. Being noticed is also enjoyable when it results in favorable and widespread publicity. Such things appeal to our pride, often result in rewards, and demonstrate that what we have been doing has been worthwhile.

Other than doing a spectacular job, what does it take to be noticed? Here are a few other ways you can bring yourself to the attention of others:

1. Accept a bad situation when everyone else is complaining. Smile to show that it is not all that bad.

2. Show that you are not discouraged and still have hope when others lose faith and decide to quit.

3. Step forward and offer your services when volunteers are requested for a tedious or distasteful job.

4. Do a bit extra when nobody else is doing more than is asked of them.

5. Always be on time or early to start your work. Of course, you'll be noticed when you're late, but this is not the notice that you want.

6. Change the time or the day on which you usually do a job.

The way to be noticed is to be different in the way you look at life and its problems compared to how other people view these things. You need not be the only one in a group to show courage, hope, and ambition. There probably will be others with you, and your actions may cause still others to change their minds. For this also, you might be noticed.

How to Be an Expert at Persuasion

If you wish to be persuasive, you must be gentle. The more disagreeable you are and the more demanding you seem, the less persuasive you are because such an approach puts a person on the defensive and tends to make him believe he is being forced to do as you ask. He should not be made to feel that he has no choice. Approaching someone calmly lets him think and reason, thereby making him easier to persuade.

Although you may feel you are successful at your job, if people do not respect you, you are at a great disadvantage. Without respect, fear and force may be your only means of getting things accomplished. Being respected makes it easier for you to persuade others.

Each of us sees things differently at various times because our mood, our temperament, and our physical and mental conditions change. Someone is at his best in the morning, while someone else is at his peak in the afternoon or evening. The secret to getting along with people, persuading them to your thinking, is to understand these differences and act accordingly.

Hector Montez, office manager of Imperial Industries, knew which of his clerks were "day" people and which were "night" people.

He carefully handed out assignments early in the morning, preferring to work with the "day" people then. Later in the day he didn't hesitate to hand out tough assignments to the "night" people.

Some people prefer not to do much talking in the morning until they've had their cup of coffee or their cigarette. Remember that it is difficult to change such people. You may as well go along with their desires as much as possible if you wish to be on good terms with them.

How to Change Attitudes

Psychologists believe that to persuade someone to change his attitude you must use both reason and emotion—and that you must use *both* techniques in almost all situations to be truly effective. However, you may need to use one more than the other depending on the individual you wish to persuade.

Dr. Frederick G. Sawyer, President & Consultant, Frederick G. Sawyer & Associates, Pasadena, California, feels that persuasion involves more than seeing that your communication gets the attention of the right people, and showing the right people that your communication is relevant to their needs and motives. He maintains that human behavior is complex and that you should never forget that your proposal may succeed or fail because of *people*—their reactions and feelings —rather than a dispassionate evaluation of your facts and figures.

The more intelligent your listener, the more you should rely on facts, logic, and reason. The less intelligent your listener, the more you should appeal to emotion. Intelligent people more easily reach conclusions on their own and need not have consequences pointed out to them.

How to Sell Benefits

You like to know how you will be affected by something that is proposed. So does the other fellow. But it is human nature to think first of oneself. So when you are selling yourself, your services, or your product, you must point out what's in it for the other fellow.

A salesman tries to get his prospective customer to appreciate the importance of certain features of his product. He does this by pointing out how the features are of help to the customer. For example, a radio salesman might say ". . . and this model has a separate on-off switch so that you don't have to adjust the volume each time you turn it on."

"What's in it for me?" is the thought that comes to someone's mind when he is asked to do something. If you wish to get others to agree with you, it's up to you to satisfactorily answer that question. Moreover, you should do so without being asked.

When you ask someone to do things for you, mention the benefits that he can gain, especially if those benefits solve one of his problems, make his life easier, or contribute to his advancement. For instance, you might say, "This will give the 'big boss' a chance to see some of your work," or, "You'll get some experience that will help you when you're moved up a grade."

Bob Todman, engineering manager, was able to sell his plant manager on assigning two of the plant's engineering people to doing preventive maintenance work exclusively. He did this by pointing out how a preventive maintenance program would greatly reduce major equipment breakdowns and thereby obtain greater productivity from the plant's equipment. Since equipment breakdowns had always been a problem in the plant, the plant manager was quick to agree to Bob's proposal. While Bob's objective was to reduce his department's costs, he sold his idea by showing his boss how the plant would benefit over and above lower maintenance costs.

How to Answer to Being Wrong

Nobody is always right. If you feel that you seldom, if ever, make a bad decision, or if your people never convince you that you're wrong, then your people aren't very observant or are afraid to speak up to you.

Of course, the correct way to handle being wrong is to willingly admit it and accept the blame. But many people find this difficult to do.

Earl Nightingale, noted writer, broadcaster, and philosopher, says, "If you believe what the majority tells you, you will be wrong most of the time, for the one thing the great majority of people will fight hardest to keep is their ignorance. Most people would rather appear absurd than admit they are wrong."

There will always be occasions when you are very sure that you are right. What should you do when someone disagrees with you?

Jack Peterson, head of his own plastics fabricating plant in Chicago, says, "It's happened that I was positive I was right when I was dead wrong. Fortunately, ever since I started suggesting that I could be wrong when I'm confronted, it's easier to admit it when I'm proved wrong."

When you make a mistake or error, you should make the correction yourself instead of letting someone else do it. You'll find that it's much less embarrassing that way; you'll also show others that you are honest and not trying to get away with something. You may as well also be pleasant about it. Such things are remembered.

How to Handle Moods

Moods affect everyone, but if you wish to be an effective leader you will not let your mood show, be it good or bad. The reason for this is that people will know when you'll say "Yes" and when you'll say "No." They'll time their actions and performance to fit your mood.

A good mood is no better than a poor one if it causes you to overlook poor performance and let things slide. Being in a good frame of mind at one time may get you in trouble in that you may allow someone to do something which you forbade someone else to do when you weren't at your best.

A good mood one day doesn't cancel out a poor one the day before. Your decisions should be based on facts, not on your mood at the moment. This is the only way you can be consistent.

Uniform treatment of individuals under similar conditions shows dependability and fairness on the part of a leader. Your mood should not be a factor. Your people will show more respect for you if you demonstrate that you are fair at all times, not just when you are feeling good.

4

How to Get Through to Others on What Must Be Done

The worth of a man on the job is determined by his ability to get along with people and his ability to get things done. Lack of either of these skills seriously handicaps him and prevents him from being a successful leader or manager.

Managers get things done through other people. To be proficient in this, they must get through to others on what must be done. But they need help to do this. Communication among people must go in more than one direction—the path is a two-way street. A leader needs to be kept informed by his people, and in order for this to occur, the leader must make it easy for his people to communicate with him.

How to Get Started on Communicating

If your people do not seem to be understanding you, or if you sense that they are not sure of what needs to be done, then you probably need to improve your communicating skill. It may be merely a matter of getting started.

When Robert Anderson was a newly-appointed manager of the Wiebolt Company he was criticized for sending out a flurry of memos on various minor matters as soon as he took over. Anderson justified his action by saying that if he didn't get some of these small things handled at once, he probably would continue to put up with them the same as his predecessor had.

Look at your job as if you had just begun it. What would you do first to get started right with your people? Now look back a bit. Are there some things that you should have handled a long time ago but have never asked that they be done? Are some of your people doing their job inefficiently because you haven't taken the time to point out how they could work more effectively? All that may be needed for you to change these things is for you to get started on *communicating*.

How to Make Your Message Clear

People hear what they want to hear. If you do not make your message clear, you may not be understood. Each individual has a different background, and therefore thinks and behaves differently from others. Consequently, he "understands" a message as it seems logical to him, based on his knowledge and experience.

Here are four suggestions on how to make your messages clear:

1. Give plenty of thought to what you are going to say beforehand so that you do not omit some important point. Plan to use words and language your listener will understand.

2. Consider giving background information and history to lead up to your message. This presents a bigger picture to the listener and acquaints him with the subject more fully.

3. Tell him why you are informing him of this and why you made a certain decision. Reasons for actions satisfy questions that listeners may have.

4. Give your message in steps if it is long or complicated. Breaking it into steps makes it easier to understand.

You improve your chance of getting through to others on what must be done if you take the time to make your message clear.

Why Completeness Is Necessary

As a leader, it's up to you to make sure your communications are understood and interpreted correctly. One way is to be sure your message is complete. When a message is incomplete people are inclined to complete it so that it makes sense to them. But in doing so, they often come to the wrong conclusion.

Another danger in not making your message complete is that what is left unsaid tends to seed rumors. People jump to various conclusions when they do not have all the facts.

The Ace Plastic Company decided to build a new plant in southern Illinois. Employees in the Chicago plant first learned of the plan when an engineering firm hired to do the design work came into the plant to study equipment layout and utility requirements. When the engineers reported to the president that employees were asking questions about the new plant, he decided that he should inform his people about his plans. He did this with a short announcement on the company bulletin board. Unfortunately, he was very brief and left many questions unanswered.

The plant in Chicago had done fairly well, but the employees knew that recent increases in taxes and an argument with the city over utility rates had irked the president.

Rumors about the new plant began among the employees. Many of the workers felt that the Chicago plant would soon be shut down and they would lose their jobs. Some even began looking for other work. In general, there was an uneasiness which affected the employees' morale and output.

When the president finally realized that his people were greatly concerned about their jobs, he told them that the new plant would manufacture only one product, demand for which had greatly increased recently. The Chicago plant would continue to operate without change. While the employees were relieved, most could not understand why the president had not made that news known earlier.

How to Get an Idea Across

As a leader you may often be faced with getting people to willingly accept an idea. You may also have trouble in explaining what must be done and why it should be done. Yet, you need to know how to do these things if you are going to be a success at your job.

If you can talk about something that interests your listener or present the part of an idea that will result in a benefit for him, you will be more likely to get his acceptance. Otherwise, he may not listen to your ideas or, if he does, he soon forgets them. Although an idea you want to put across may be a company goal, you must present it in a way in which your listener can make it his goal, also. For example, you should point out the possibility (or probability) of greater earnings, easier work, better working conditions, or more security. Sell him and you will get your idea across more easily.

Written communications are good for passing basic information, especially when one must refer to the information frequently. Nobody can be expected to learn and remember schedules, prices, locations, and similar data. But written communications may be inadequate for much other information. Putting a message in writing doesn't guarantee that everyone will understand it.

While someone may not hesitate to ask a question when he receives information orally, he may be reluctant to show that he does not understand something he receives in writing. He may not wish to go to the trouble to ask. To avoid the possibility of such happening, you should follow up your written messages with conversation. The easy way to do this is to simply ask, "Do you have any questions about . . . ?" or, "Did you have a chance to read my note about . . . ?"

Periodic meetings with your people to keep them informed of company plans and their effect on your people pay off. You show your interest in the workers and their future. When the time comes for you to put an idea across they will be more receptive if they have confidence in you.

How to Get People to Listen

In general, people do not know how to listen. Immediately after the average individual has listened to someone he remembers only about half of what he heard, regardless of how carefully he tried to listen. Worse, two months later he will remember only about 25 percent of what was said.

If we could get people to always listen carefully we could improve our communications and be much more effective leaders. What can you do to make your people better listeners?

You can help if you can get them in the right mental attitude for listening, as well as make them aware of the factors that affect listening. You can tell someone how to do these things and show them the advantages of being a good listener. But before you try to do this, here's how to become a better listener yourself.

Seven Ways to Become a Better Listener

You can become a better listener by learning what procedures are involved and then practicing those procedures as you listen. Here is what you should do:

1. Be ready to listen. Put aside other things you have been doing or thinking about. Prepare yourself by being alert in your posture and face.

2. Try to avoid distractions. Distractions come in many forms, and extreme concentration may be needed to shut them out. The most common distraction is noise, such as other voices or sounds. The speaker himself may be a distraction; he may have an accent which makes his words difficult to understand, or he may have disturbing mannerisms such as removing and putting on his glasses, jingling coins in his pocket, or moving about.

3. Eliminate bias and prejudice in your thoughts. Try not to be influenced by personal feelings toward the speaker or his subject. Look past the dramatic, emotional side of the speaker to what he is saying.

4. Think about what the speaker is saying. What is the meaning of his words? Try to anticipate what he will say next and how he will say it. Guess what his conclusions will be, and decide if you agree or disagree with him. This kind of thinking will ward off boredom if the speaker or the subject matter is dull.

5. Listen for the speaker's ideas as he talks. Determine what points he is trying to make and if he has reasons to back them up. Organize his opinions in order of importance, both from his viewpoint and yours. Try not to memorize figures unless they are repeated because you want to retain the broad meaning of his message, not the details. Periodically summarize what you have heard whenever you have time between the speaker's words.

6. Separate the advantages and disadvantages of the speaker's message. You will then find it easy to evaluate his words as you try to reach your own conclusions. Grouping ideas or points will make it easier to remember them.

7. Look for and remember the speaker's *key* words. You can easily recall his supporting words and arguments if you have outlined his message using such keys. Some speakers jump back and forth in their talks, not having carefully organized what they have to say. You will not be confused by this if you have picked out key words.

Similarly, separate the essential words from those not related to the subject. Often a speaker may ramble or add words which he doesn't need to make his point. By ignoring these you can concentrate on his main ideas.

If you follow these procedures you can keep your mind on what is being said and your thoughts will not wander to other things. As a result you will be a much better listener.

How Being a Good Listener Pays Off

Being a good listener will increase your knowledge and make you better informed. However, there are other reasons for you to want to improve your listening skills.

You will get along much better with people if you understand what they say; you will be closer to them and understand their feelings more fully. Your relationships with friends and family will be more pleasant if *they* know you will listen to them.

Business employees must understand one another and their superiors if operations are to be efficient. No company wants dissatisfied customers because of errors in numbers, dates, and locations. Such errors often are caused by poor listening.

Tom Casey realized that his superior, W. A. Watson, felt strongly about reports expected from his section heads, both as to their content and when they were due. The tone of voice Watson used when he opened the monthly meeting told Tom that he expected compliance.

Sensing this, Tom listened carefully during the meeting and made notes immediately afterward on what he was expected to report.

His care paid off. A few weeks later, Watson complimented him on having submitted the most comprehensive and complete report of those he had received from the section heads.

Get your people to work toward being better listeners. Only a little time and effort are needed for a lot to be gained. The good listener is more efficient and is admired for his knowledge.

How Listening Affects Human Relations

People need to be able to talk to their leaders and to know that they will be heard and understood. But too many leaders fail to listen. As a result, they fail to communicate.

When people do not talk about their problems, those problems often become worse, affecting their job and their relations with their boss. Attitudes change for the worse; efficiency and motivation also suffer. Better listening can reduce the problems of people getting along with each other.

For example, there may be times on the job when a worker may start making more mistakes or fail to get much done. An unsympathetic supervisor may be too quick to criticize or reprimand the worker when he should instead take him aside, talk to him, and really listen to what he has to say. There is a reason for abnormal behavior. A leader who takes the time to talk and listen to someone who has a problem may be able to help him. At least he will understand enough to avoid taking action which might be improper or for which he might be sorry later.

Before you give your people what *you* think they want or what *you* think would be good for them, find out first what *they* really want.

Bob Smith, superintendent of the South Bend plant of National Brass Co., couldn't understand why the men in the Molding Department didn't express their thanks to him when he went through the shop the day after he had authorized a 7¢/hour wage increase for them. Finally he decided to bring up the subject with a couple of the old-timers. The answers he got surprised him.

"Heck, we'd much rather you'd made the shop a better place to work in. We've complained to the foremen—we need better ventilation and the lighting is poor. Why don't you get some good exhaust fans? Can't you afford to put in some more lights in the pour area? Management around here just doesn't seem to care about the employees.''

Do you listen to your people when they tell you what they want or need on the job?

How Listening Gains Support

Labor relations experts believe that management people talk too much and listen too little. ''What employees want most is not money but a systematic and effective procedure to voice their gripes, grievances, and suggestions. They want to be heard,'' emphasizes A. A. Imberman of the management consulting firm of Imberman & DeForest, Chicago. ''The supervisors who seem to have the most wholehearted support of their workers—who can motivate the workers to do more than the minimum and produce better quality products—are those who don't just wait for the worker complaints and suggestions to come to them, but rather go out and make themselves available to workers, and listen.

''Management always has the first chance to listen to such complaints and to deal with them,'' Mr. Imberman declares, ''but if management has no procedure for listening to employees, union organizers readily lend a sympathetic ear.''

Gain the support of your people by listening to them. There is no better way to learn their feelings and their needs. The fact that you will take the time to listen shows that you are interested in them. People are more willing to work for someone when they know they are appreciated.

How to Start Conversations

Have you ever had someone approach you with a question such as, ''Are you going to do it?'' At the moment, you are ''lost'' because you don't know about what the speaker is talking. It may take you a few seconds to think back to recent conversations or events to which the speaker may be referring. If it doesn't come to you quickly you may need to ask him. But nobody likes to ask ''Am I going to do what?''

Your inability to immediately understand a question like this is caused by failure on the part of the other fellow to say a few words on the subject before he asks his question. Because of this failure you are unable to associate his words with a previous incident.

You probably have been guilty of this on some occasion and not realized it. You may have been thinking about a subject and assumed your listener was doing the same. Or the last few words of your earlier conversation with him may have suggested that you would be asking the question when you next met.

Nevertheless, you and your listener can avoid this situation which makes both of you appear mentally unalert in the eyes of each other. All the speaker need do is say a few introductory words on the subject to get his listener tuned in and thinking along the same line. For example, as a prelude to his question, the speaker could say, "This decision you are going to make about hiring another man, are you . . . ?" or perhaps, "I'm interested in your problem of needing more help in your department. Have you . . . ?"

The next time you are going to ask someone a question, help him to get on the track with you by giving him a few lead up words. You'll appear more intelligent in his eyes, as well as save him the embarrassment of not immediately understanding you and having to tell you so.

How to Communicate Through Praise

By praising someone you make him more receptive to requests you will make of him. He is more willing and likely to communicate, also, if his ego has been satisfied.

Many people shy away from using praise. They find it difficult to do because they fear that they will be considered insincere. Others may worry that they may be accused of using it to gain an advantage. Some people think that a recipient of praise may expect more liberties or more pay; this is not usually true.

In a survey at Texas Foundries, Inc., the employees were asked, "Do men who are praised for good work usually expect more pay?" The answers were: 11 percent, "Yes," 89 percent, "No." The survey revealed: "Men expect more pay if they are doing a good job and have shown improvement in their work. They do not expect more pay whenever they are praised. They want to be complimented for good work. They also want to know when they are not doing well. Raises should be based on merit, experience, time on the job, and company's ability to pay."

Someone who has been praised feels the obligation to respond, whether it be a simple "thanks" or a compliment in return. Often the response is not oral, but shows itself in a noticeable increase in enthusiasm for the job or willingness to cooperate.

You will find that you can get through to others on what must be done more easily if you have prefaced your approach by praise for what already has been done. "Big Joe" Wilson, construction foreman for the Acme Co. in Houston, often uses this technique when giving assignments to his men on the job. He learned that his men appreciate a good word on the work they did the day before. If he has talked about some of the unusual jobs they are also less likely to proceed on questionable work without discussing it with him beforehand.

If you are not already using praise in communicating, you should add it to your leadership skills. Try it to see how it improves your relations with your people.

How to Give Effective Instructions

One of the most important parts of the job of managing or directing people is to see that they are productive and that they do work in the right manner. Even enthusiastic and efficient people need direction and guidance if their efforts are to be fully utilized. Frequently the determinant of how much gets done is up to the leader and the effectiveness of his instructions.

It would seem that explaining a job or asking for something to be done would be simple. Yet for many people this can be difficult and tension-producing. Some may fear that there will be misunderstandings and bad feelings, others may worry that the job may not be done correctly or get done at all.

You can learn how to give instructions so that jobs are handled promptly, work gets done correctly, and people get satisfaction from accomplishment.

Initially you must know what makes you effective and also be aware of what makes you ineffective. You must understand the person or people you are instructing. You must know the problem or job to be handled. Finally, you must "put together" all this knowledge to make your approach suitable to the time, the place, the individual, and the task.

Gordon Leavy, a plant manager of one of the large steel companies, encountered a communications problem and was able to contend with it to the benefit of the organization. A governmental agency had issued new regulations and standards for environmental control for his industry. These standards and compliance instructions were sent to Gordon from the company law department. Although he understood the regulations and how his company intended to abide by them, he knew that he could not simply pass the instructions as he had received them to the operating people. The technical language in which the regulations were presented, as well as the lack of detail on how to meet them, precluded that they would not be adequately nor satisfactorily met. Gordon therefore wisely assigned to his technical department the task of putting the regulations into a Plant Operating Specification which contained procedures written in a form which was readily understandable by the plant operating people.

When a government inspector toured the plant a few months later, he was so impressed by how well the regulations were being followed that he recommended the company for an award. In appreciation, Gordon was named company vice-president.

Three Steps for Giving Instructions

Three basic steps are involved in giving effective instructions. Your degree of success depends on how well you handle each.

1. Preparing
2. Instructing
3. Following up

Let's look at each of these individually.

How to Prepare for Giving Instructions

You can be much more effective in giving instructions if you take some time beforehand for planning. Here are several suggestions on how to do this:

1. Consider the timing of what you wish to say. The occurrence of other events may make one time poor for giving instructions while some time in the future may be more appropriate.

2. Decide when you want to have your instructions carried out. If preliminary preparation is required on the part of the person doing the work you should allow for this.

3. Know the best way to do the job so that when you explain you will be prepared to answer any detailed questions on procedure.

4. Select where the job should be done. Know where tools and materials are to be found. Checking out these details beforehand avoids confusion and delay. It also enables you to give a complete story without leaving any part undecided.

5. Try to compile all the facts about the job. Gathering relevant information helps to avoid overlooking some details.

6. Study what you are going to explain. Be satisfied that your instructions will be precise, not omitting any necessary information nor adding any that would be unnecessary. The latter may only confuse your listener.

7. Decide whom you are going to ask to carry out your instructions. Some people need more instructions than others. If more than one person is involved, you may need to be specific about who does what.

8. Consider how much your listener already knows about what you are going to cover. Beware of assuming that his knowledge is very broad and that he is experienced.

9. Try to use simple words and short sentences. Avoid the technical language (jargon) which your listener may not understand.

10. Be sure you are not prejudiced or biased in your instructions. Your listener may be offended or influenced unfairly.

11. Plan to pause and listen when giving instructions to allow your listener time to think, absorb what you are saying, and perhaps ask a question.

12. Decide whether the help of another person will be of benefit to

you. The backing or presence of someone your listener respects may add credence to what you have to say.

13. Plan where you are going to give your instructions. Should it be in your office, at the listener's work place, or away from the job? Each place is psychologically different in its effect on the receptiveness and understanding of the listener. Many people are fearful and ill-at-ease when asked to come to the boss' office. Thus, this may be one of the poorest places.

How to Instruct

The ways you use to instruct greatly influence your effectiveness. For example, you should give your listener a chance to ask questions. You should consider emotions and point out benefits. Let's look at several of these and other ways you can help yourself when giving instructions.

Your Tone of Voice Is Important

How you get through to your listener is determined by the tone of your voice. If you are scolding or critical you may cause resentment—if you appear to be joking you may create an over-relaxed atmosphere —and if you are serious, you indicate that what you are saying is very important.

A demanding voice should be used sparingly, if at all. Almost everybody dislikes someone who demands: first, because he displays authority, and people like to feel equal or superior; second, because he implies there will be unpleasant consequences if there is no compliance.

Tact Makes a Difference

Giving instructions without hurting someone's feelings is an art which makes the job of getting things done a real challenge. It involves knowing what to say, when to say it, and how to say it. Your choice of words makes a difference as does your body and facial appearance.

The good manager or leader doesn't *demand* that something be done—he *asks* for something to be done. Although he still expects compliance, the worker being asked feels differently about it; he senses he has a choice (even though he may not). Also, the boss-worker relationship is softened and put more on an equal basis when instructions are put in the form of requests.

Commands and direct orders should be used only under unusual conditions such as an emergency or when quick action will prevent an accident or loss.

How to Make Your Instructions Understood

By giving instructions that are easily understood, you minimize the possibility of mistakes. You also gain the respect and confidence of your listener because he will realize you know what you are talking about.

Put your listener in a good frame of mind before you give him instructions. How? Inquire about his family, his hobby, or how he is feeling. Ask him how his work is going. By asking a question or two you can determine his attitude and emotional state at the moment. Learning this helps in choosing your tone and how you give your instructions to ensure his agreement and acceptance.

Here are ways to make it easy for your listener to understand you:

1. Talk at a speed which allows your listener time to understand but not to become impatient. Watch your listener for telltale signs to avoid being too fast or too slow.

2. Speak with the right volume for the closeness of your listener and the noise in the area. Pronounce your words carefully.

3. Break up complicated and lengthy instructions into smaller steps.

4. Give instructions in logical order if they involve several steps.

5. Be consistent. If you call something by a certain name at one time, use the same name when you refer to it later.

6. Avoid discrimination. If one person must do a job in a prescribed manner, all other persons asked to do that job must do it likewise.

7. Slant your instructions to what your listener already knows and

understands. Give examples. Compare what you are saying to something similar that he already knows.

8. Make sure you fully understand a question before you reply, even if you have to ask a question of your own.

9. Explain why a job is being done. People more easily understand and find the work more interesting if they know the reason for the work and why a certain procedure is followed.

How to Handle Questions

Some people think that if they dominate a conversation, others will be overwhelmed and must concede to the speaker's desires. They fear that the listener may have objections or disagree, so they try to repress him with a lot of facts and fast talk.

It doesn't work out that way. For one thing, it's poor psychology to overpower someone whose help and cooperation you need since you risk losing these things. For another, you must give the other fellow the opportunity to have his say and let you know how he feels, because he will have a better opinion of you for that opportunity.

You may think that any question your listener might have could only be minor or of little consequence. On the contrary, his question is important to him and, at the moment, his main concern. You must satisfy him or you may not get the cooperation you need.

Another point about questions from your listener—you should prefer to have them asked rather than have him remain silent. Having questions asked shows interest, tells you whether you have been understood, and lets you know if you have agreement.

How to Overcome Obstacles

Obstacles often stand in the way when instructions are given. You must overcome them to be effective. Obstacles consist of emotion and reason.

Emotion must always be dealt with first since logic will fail when your listener is emotional. The best way to contend with emotion is to concede that your listener has a right to his opinion and that he may be correct. You must also stop talking yourself and listen. Only after you have learned why your listener is negative can you go about trying to persuade him to change his thinking.

You may still need to let your listener "work off" his emotion after you learn what is behind his objection. When he realizes you are trying to see his viewpoint, he will be more willing to discuss his difference in opinion, and you may then be able to resolve the problem.

You will find that people will be more willing and do a better job if they can feel that they are helping to get something done or contributing to reach a goal. This is why it is so important to let them know why the job is being done. People like to feel *in* on things, even when they are not directly involved.

Some people resent authority. They dislike having to take orders from someone. They would like to be their own boss, decide for themselves how a job should be done, and pick their own rate of speed to do it.

Try to go along with such people as much as possible. It is better to have an agreeable fellow doing a job than one who is unhappy, reluctant, or belligerent. The happy fellow will do a better and faster job.

Watch Your Own Mood and Temperament

Avoid being sarcastic when you give instructions. Your listener may not understand why you are in this mood and may resent such treatment. Sarcasm certainly will not cause him to do a better job.

Losing your temper also does not help to get things done. It may cause someone else to lose his and thereby result in an argument. Angry people do not get things done. When you are angry the instructions you give will not be your best because your emotions will affect them. Your listener may also misunderstand the meaning of words said in anger.

Be considerate and reasonable in what you expect someone to do for you. Requesting a large amount of work to be done in a short period of time may cause people to think you unfair. It is better to challenge someone to do as much as he can of the job with periodic encouragement and praise for what he has accomplished. The unreasonable approach can cause gripes and complaints which cut short available work time.

How Positive and Optimistic Instructions Pay Off

Positive instructions are always better than negative ones. Tell someone the *right* way to do a job rather than tell him not to do it the wrong way.

Several benefits arise from giving positive instructions. Your listener responds more favorably to a positive viewpoint, making it easier for him to understand. Ethics make it easier to sell a positive idea than a negative one. When you instruct positively, you are more persuasive—what you say is more credible and authoritative. Also, your listener has more respect for you if your attitude is positive.

Give your instructions in a manner which creates and maintains pleasant relations with your listener. Being sympathetic, considerate, enthusiastic, and cheerful influences people emotionally to be that way themselves.

When you wish to stress the importance of your instructions you can convey this thought by being concerned, serious, earnest, and thoughtful. Remember, though, that your listener will perceive and accept the manner of your instructions only if you are sincere.

A friendly and confident "I-know-you-can-do-it" attitude will get your instructions accepted and carried out faster than the pessimistic "this-is-probably-too-tough-for-you" approach. Along the same lines, a smile instead of a frown, and patience rather than anxiety will get more things done faster in the long run. Be interested in instead of indifferent to how your listener feels.

By complimenting someone, you make him more attentive and receptive to future instructions. Of course, the compliment must be sincere and must concern an accomplishment that the listener is proud of.

Appealing to someone's pride is particularly effective when his ego needs boosting. If you achieve this, you please him emotionally, and he will more willingly accept instructions.

How to Instruct by Presenting Ideas

If you can give your instructions in the form of ideas, asking your listener's opinion, you appeal to his judgment and ability. For example, ask, "What do you think of this?" or, "Would it work if you . . . ?" or, "I suppose you thought of . . ." or, "Have you tried . . . ?"

What if someone thinks your idea was his idea? Good! Let him continue to think so. There is no harm in doing this especially if his ego is given a lift, as it will be.

Presenting ideas and asking your listener to respond helps to get him interested. It also gives him the feeling that his opinion is important and that he is helping make decisions.

The foreman in the plant who approaches his people with "Let's try . . ." gives them an opportunity to think about and participate in solving problems.

How to Point out Benefits When Instructing

If you can point out benefits when you give instructions you will show your listener "what's in it for him." The way to do this is to mention his gain as well as yours in the same statement. For instance, you might tell one of your workers that the quality of the product he is working on will be better, the work will go easier, and he will be safer if he uses the right tools.

Pointing out benefits results in better attitude, more cooperation, and higher productivity. However, you must be sure that the benefits you talk about are real to both you and your listener.

You can improve your effectiveness in giving instructions by showing your listener what harm could occur if your directions are not followed. Explain what could happen, such as an accident or a spoiled product, if a job is done improperly.

To avoid the possibility that your listener will think that you are critical of him or may blame him, refrain from using the word "you" in such explanations. Saying that "anyone" or "everyone" would fail if the wrong procedure is followed does not give the listener the impression that *he* is guilty or erring in his work.

How to Follow-up

Following-up to see that your instructions have been understood and are being carried out is the third step in being effective in giving instructions. It pays to follow-up before your instructions are completely carried out.

An efficient manager or leader periodically inquires how the job is going and if additional help is needed. He shows an interest throughout the progress of a job and is ready to solve problems if they arise. Praise for what has been accomplished is always in order. Whoever is carrying out your instructions appreciates such words on your part since they let him know that you are aware of his efforts and how he is doing. The offering of encouragement as a job progresses also helps to get your instructions carried out faster and better. Again, the fact that you are interested enough to offer such words shows your concern.

How to Know When Your Instructions Are Not Effective

It's usually very easy to learn when your instructions are not effective. Simply, the work does not get done in a reasonable time, or it is not done properly, or you see a poor attitude among those you instructed. At the worst, you might meet outright refusal to do the work.

If you get such results you, of course, need to learn why. If you are at fault you want to be able to correct yourself as well as do better next time.

Determine if you should have planned better or if you overlooked something. Go over how you gave your instructions. Decide if your follow-up was weak. If you cannot see any reasons, consider asking someone for their opinion. You want to know so that you can make your instructions more effective in the future.

How to Help People to Be Successful

People's worth on the job depends on how they do their work, as well as how they get along with others. You can help them in both efforts by making sure they understand what is required of them and by strengthening and promoting their human relations. By giving good instructions you help people to be successful and to enjoy their work.

The good qualities of people should be mentioned to them. They will be pleased to hear that their actions are noticed and appreciated. Virtues such as ambition, honesty, courage, and cooperation help to make people successful. Through being successful, people become satisfied and happy. And that, after all, is what makes life worth living.

5

How to Get Your People
to Plan Ahead

Some form of planning is carried out in all successful organizations. Everyone, from the top executive down to the worker on the job, must, to some extent, plan. While some of management's plans may be for years ahead and very general in nature, the current year's plans may be quite specific and detailed.

Although planning is a human trait and is practiced to some degree by almost everybody, we usually don't like to do it. It's difficult and often tedious, and it requires extra thought. Too, we fear the unknown, what the future might bring. We also don't like to take chances. We overlook the fact that doing nothing is still making a decision. But planning *is* necessary and becomes more so every day if we are to grow and improve ourselves.

The best way to get your people to plan is to set an example for them. Plan your own work and involve your people in your plans. Discuss with them why they need to prepare for the future and the advantages of doing so.

To demonstrate your sincere belief in planning, make your plans known publicly. By going on record with your superiors and your subordinates you show an awareness of what needs to be done. Also, you provide a stimulus for action.

Why Planning Is Necessary

Man has always wondered about the future. The challenge of being able to accurately predict what will happen, while never totally met, has pushed him to do the best he can in planning and preparing for the unknown. And he has been better off through such efforts. Companies that plan have fared much better than ones that don't in this very competitive business world.

Why is planning important? Through planning we decide a course of action to achieve goals and accomplish objectives. Too, planning enables us to go about satisfying our needs.

We must know how to perform in the event that certain things happen—we must know what we will do under certain circumstances. But most of all, we need steps to follow to make our company profitable and to move ahead.

Establishing company policy is a part of planning since policy dictates course of action. Company policy should always be clear and understandable so that people involved with planning can carry out their work with confidence and assurance.

Operating a paint manufacturing plant where the product line is continually changing and equipment runs 24-hours-a-day requires good planning and scheduling to keep equipment operating and costs under control. Oscar Boswell, the new operations manager of such a plant in St. Louis, inherited a situation in which planning had been poor and costs very high. He worked closely with his managers on plant problems, meeting each morning to go over the previous 24 hours of plant performance and to plan upcoming operations. Three departmental functions were discussed: production, control and quality, and maintenance and engineering. Although frequently having a choice of courses to follow, they worked to find the best way to produce quality products at lowest cost. To control cost, which is always difficult, Oscar insisted that everyone be very specific in how jobs were to be handled, since each one contributed to the total cost of operation. Within a year, costs had dropped 42 percent, and Oscar received a salary increase of $7,000 a year.

How Planning Varies

Planning can be short-range or long-range. Generally, planning for only a few months or a year is easier and likely to be more accurate than trying to look several years ahead. However, even long-range planning by competent businessmen has been surprisingly accurate. Whenever this planning has not succeeded it has been due mostly to underestimating.

Many companies are satisfied with plans which will carry them through the next year or two. The current figures of production and cost are with what management is most concerned. They want to see a satisfactory return and payout from the decisions they make today.

People who do much planning are often more successful if they have imagination as well as some creative ability. Having a proper balance of optimism and pessimism—and a practical plus realistic viewpoint—also helps. Such traits are an aid since planning involves forecasting, and although mathematical, economic, and statistical techniques are employed in forecasting, all are frequently tempered with human intuition.

Ten Reasons for Planning

Many advantages arise from planning. Here are the most important:

1. The act of planning requires getting facts and data, procedures which enable good decisions to be made currently as well as in the future. The more information available to a leader, the better-equipped he is to make correct decisions.

2. Standards and specifications are originated when planning. If some of these already exist, then they are examined and brought up-to-date. The procedure results in tightening controls and smoother transition from decision-making to execution.

3. Organizational objectives are reviewed under planning proce-

dures. A redirecting of course often results, along with more emphasis being placed on basic company objectives.

4. Planning usually involves most members of an organization, thus unifying them in a common effort. The melding of thinking is achieved with understanding of the direction in which the company expects to move and the defining of responsibilities of individuals.

5. Change is more easily accepted throughout the organization when plans are known. Delays and lost time are minimized when understandings exist. There need be no hesitation in execution.

6. Getting everyone involved in planning brings improved communications within the organization. With originating proposals, suggestions, and recommendations, both horizontal and vertical exchange of information take place.

7. Planning causes management to more thoroughly investigate opportunities for action. Such opportunities may concern remodeling, expansion, and introduction of new facilities or product lines.

8. Planning calls attention to dangers and pitfalls. Disadvantages will also be uncovered with every advantage the company can foresee from a particular plan if the planning is thorough.

9. The procedure of planning helps to develop managers in the art of decision-making. If several courses of action are possible for a particular problem, the decision-maker must consider the probable outcome of each. His skill in making decisions is thus enhanced.

10. The large number of variables and factors to be considered in decision-making are put in proper perspective when planning. Two benefits result: recognition of all the factors, and assignment of proper weight to each.

While leaders may recognize the need and advantages of planning, they must also see that the plans they make will be easy to carry out.

How to Make a Good Plan

What are the requirements of a good plan? Any plan which facilitates decision-making should have these features:

1. It must be specific rather than general. Objectives must be clearly defined. Means of implementation should be indicated.

2. Discrimination should be shown between the known and the unknown so that both may be viewed in the proper perspective. The probable effects of the unknown should be estimated. Planning should have a greater depth than mere anticipation.

3. The plan must be logical and based on facts, whenever possible. If facts are not available, then reasonable, sound judgments must be made. Intelligent behavior leads to logical plans.

4. The plan must be acceptable to the individuals who put it in effect and to those who are affected. Acceptability means willingness to cooperate and participate.

5. The plan must be flexible. No plan can cover all contingencies, nor do conditions under which a plan will operate always remain constant. It must be easy to change a plan if necessary.

Planning removes most of the doubt as to what the company expects to do in the future and how it will be done. All people perform more efficiently when definite courses are laid out for them to follow. Teamwork is more evident and cooperation prevails when individuals work toward a common goal.

Why People Resist Change

People resist change for several reasons, but behind most you'll find fear, whether it be real or imagined. People feel that whatever change brings may result in a worse situation than presently exists. But if you know the reasons why people resist change you may be able to lower that resistance, reduce their fears, and thus make change more acceptable.

For example, someone may resist change because he interprets its introduction as a remedy for his poor performance. He may feel that he has been inadequate and that a change is therefore being made to get more from him. He needs assurance that he is not at fault and that any change adopted will be to his advantage.

Another individual may think that he will lose some of his authority because of change. Someone may have personal rather than impersonal reasons to resist change.

Resistance can be expected when a change is going to require learning. The need to learn a new procedure or to become skilled in another art arouses a fear that such things cannot be easily done.

Introducing change without consulting someone beforehand or giving him an opportunity to participate in formulating it may cause a natural resistance simply because this person feels left out. "Why didn't he ask me how I felt?" or "If I had been asked, I would have suggested that . . ." are typical comments illustrating this common reaction.

Three Arguments for Change

Because it is human nature to resist change, you may need assurance to accept that change is necessary for your people to move ahead and for your company to progress. How do you avoid being an obstacle to change? Here are three views you should take to help you face the problem:

1. Forget about a seemingly comfortable situation if it's inefficient. Just because something appears to run smoothly doesn't mean it shouldn't be changed.

2. Give up the idea that old and accustomed ways of doing a job are best. Because something hasn't been changed in a long time doesn't mean it is still good.

3. Resist the temptation to immediately belittle and find fault when a new idea comes up. Give each new idea some thought or a fair trial before you discard it.

Robert L. Wooley, President, Teledyne Sprague Engineering, Cardena, California, believes that a man must have a creative streak in him in order for him to challenge discouragement. The creativity should show itself in welcoming problems as new opportunities, recognizing that old ways are no longer the most profitable, and that one must readily adapt to change.

Think about some changes that recently occurred in your job. Did you resist them at the time? How do you feel about them now? Looking back you may wonder why they worried you.

How to Plan for Change

If you plan for change it will be easier to accept. Planning also brings to light opportunities to get other things done when making a change. For instance, you may be able to get needed publicity, upgrade communications, and bolster human relations with your people.

Planning amounts to answering questions about change, and people are always involved with change; if they were not, change wouldn't be a problem. Here are some questions which need to be answered when making a change:

1. Who will be involved? Will some people be involved more than others?

2. How much will they be involved? Will the change affect their prestige, position, or pay?

3. Will the people accept the change willingly or with resistance? Will there be more resistance if the change is drastic?

4. How will the people be affected to advantage? Will the change make them feel better, make their work easier, make them more efficient?

Good planning should come from more than just technical analysis alone, but from greater emphasis on human resources, according to Norman G. Eley, University of Windsor. Good planning, he feels, depends on a tie-in between programs and people, between procedures on paper and actual operations, between planned goals and the proven abilities and desires of people.

Your plans should consider these and similar questions. As you can see, planning enables you to do a more thorough job of preparing for change. You are less likely to overlook some important detail.

The timing of a change is important. You can make it coincide with other events to advantage. You should also realize that to avoid conflict or too great a change at one time, it may be wise to spread change out in the future. When doing this, the complete plan should be known to everybody so that they can be prepared and know what to expect.

James F. Lincoln realized that he had to reduce costs in handling, storage, and inspection in his Lincoln Electric Company plant. He began asking the workers for their ideas two years before he made any changes. As a result, he encountered very little opposition or lag in production at the time of the actual changes.

How to Introduce Change

The world hates change, yet it is the only thing that has brought progress. If we could just remember this, it might be easier for us to accept change the next time that it is proposed.

Henry Ford II said, "Nobody can really guarantee the future. The best we can do is size up the chances, calculate the risks involved, estimate our ability to deal with them, and then make our plans with confidence."

Whenever you see that a change should be made, you should start preparing people for it. By reducing people's concern, you make it easier for them to accept the change when it does come.

In a large plant where many changes were planned, management tried an experiment to try to learn how best to handle them. They divided the affected workers into three groups. One group was told that there was to be a change made but there would be no decrease in pay. A second group was told *why* the change was being made and asked to help in planning it. A third group was told why the change was being made but not asked to help, but instead to cooperate.

The first group remained uncooperative and resistive. Their adjustment was slow, and almost one-fifth quit within two months. In the second group, the workers quickly adjusted and their output soon exceeded all previous records. The third group adjusted satisfactorily with no resignations, but their recovery was much slower than that of the group which had been asked to help in planning.

Letting your people know well in advance of any change you propose to make and also convincing them that they will be able to adjust easily will help you to minimize its emotional effects. But you can do even better by asking for their advice and help. Making them feel that they are participating in decision-making relative to their jobs will get you more of their support.

How to Make Change More Acceptable

Bringing about change within an organization is among the most difficult tasks of any manager. Tony Hain, an associate professor of industrial psychology at the General Motors Institute in Flint, Michigan, interviewed more than 300 General Motors plant personnel at four plants in his search for the answer of how to make change more acceptable in industrial plants.

Hain found that resistance to change was less when a respected outsider was brought in to introduce the change. His study also revealed that better results were attained when change was introduced gradually through a period of reality testing.

Both those ordering the change in upper management and those delegated to carry it out must agree on its need. When change is viewed as a necessary evil, people strongly resist it.

Hain's study also showed that middle managers resist change more than upper or lower level managers. Reasons for this seemed to be that middle managers experience frustration due to subordinates balking at carrying out unreasonable orders. Lower level managers don't fight making changes but they are concerned about lacking sufficient authority.

How to Get the Most from Change

When you have become aware that change is necessary, you must now plan how you will do it. What is the best way? How can you get the most from change?

You may as well think big and plan to go all the way. Several reasons favor such an approach:

1. By making a large change now you won't need to make additional changes later. If you're going to disrupt people and operations, it's better to do it only once and get it over with.

2. Beware of going only halfway on a change. Will you be satisfied afterward? Better that you complete it rather than be continually plagued in the future until you do.

3. You'll gain more pride from accomplishment of a big project. You'll also gain more rewards and better recognition.

4. If you are forced to revise your plans it is usually easier to cut down on a goal than to make it greater.

The career success stories you read about concern the people who weren't afraid to set far-reaching goals for themselves. By thinking big and having confidence in their abilities they were able to forge ahead of others. If you are faced with change, exploit it—get the most from it.

How Planning Can Help You Get Ahead

A good leader continually takes inventory of his people, money, and time so that he can use them in the best way possible. In doing so he plans how these assets should be applied to do a job most effectively. He knows that he needs to add to these assets the information, materials, and tools to do jobs, and that use of these things also requires his planning skill. Through planning, then, he molds all his resources to accomplish objectives and reach goals.

You can be better organized than your peers and even some of your superiors by outlining and planning your work. One way to demonstrate this to yourself is by doing a thorough job of preparing for a meeting. In most cases you know what you will be asked or expected to contribute. Being ready to report, make recommendations, and accept assignments are excellent ways to gain more responsibility and power. Planning and preparing for the meeting can enable you to do this.

Taking a few minutes each morning to plan how you will use your time that day also pays off. Decide what is your most important task and then plan to get it done before going on to other jobs. Doing first things first enables you to stay ahead of the game and minimize pressures put on you by others.

Long-term personal planning has much to say for it, especially if you put your goals in writing. The importance of this was revealed by a nationwide survey a few years ago. Only 3 percent of people interviewed had put down on paper definite plans for what they wanted to achieve in life. Another 10 percent had a general idea of what they hoped to do. The survey revealed that those with written goals had achieved ten to 100 times greater success and were independently wealthy. The 10 percent were moderately well-off. People who put their plans in writing generally follow through with them regardless of the obstacles they encounter.

Another way that planning can help you is in foreseeing and completing a task which will be asked of you. There's a great deal of satisfaction to be gained by being able to occasionally report to your superior, "I've already handled that matter," or "I thought you would be asking for this soon, so I've got it ready for you."

How Planning Helps Get Things Done

You probably respect the ability of your people to know what needs to be done and how to do it. So you may tend to leave them alone to do their work. They, in turn, may leave you alone because they feel capable of solving their own problems and know which are the most urgent jobs. As a result of not "bothering" each other, the direction and magnitude of the work being done is not nearly the quality that it could be. You can help to remedy this by scheduling and holding meetings to discuss goals and job priorities as well as communicate about new developments.

Periodic get-togethers with your people help to get things done and keep your efforts going in the right direction. "Status" meetings bring people up-to-date on progress of jobs, new goals, and priority ratings on work already in progress.

Job-oriented employees look forward to planning sessions of this type since they are interested in their company, its achievements, and its problems. Frequent planning of work renews enthusiasm and offers new challenges.

Jeff Anderson, Engineering Manager of Stanton Products, Inc., in Battle Creek, Michigan, holds a planning meeting with his section heads once a month. They meet the same day, or the day after the Plant Manager has held his Plant Council meeting which all department managers attend. With these meetings Jeff is able to let his people know without delay what jobs have top priority. As a result, they are well-informed on current problems and able to anticipate the needs of other departments which they will be called upon to satisfy.

If you are not already meeting regularly with your people to alert them to new developments and discuss your problems, you should start doing so. Your people's team spirit and cooperativeness as a department will benefit. Pressures and tensions of the job will be less through reducing the number of "surprises" sprung on you and your people.

Many manufacturing plants shut down their production lines for one or two weeks each summer. Management has found that many benefits can be realized from this practice, among them taking advantage of the equipment being idle to perform maintenance, change the process, and make new installations which could not be handled while the plant was operating. A great deal of planning goes into such efforts, with plans being made the year around. Planning enables the work to be scheduled efficiently and with considerable detail. Materials and equipment are assured to be on hand at the time, and labor is assigned to specific tasks. Frequently, management will plan more work than time and labor will permit, but always with established priorities. By such planning, the maximum is accomplished at the minimum cost.

Five Ways to Get Ideas

Getting ideas is a way of planning in which objectives are considered and ways of attaining them figured out. The man who is continually thinking is the one who gets ahead because his ideas solve problems and provide ways in which to do jobs more efficiently. He achieves goals for his company and himself, for the betterment of both.

Some people think that only the intellectual individuals, or so-called "brains," can produce ideas, but the fact is that anyone who tries to can do so, especially if his thoughts and efforts are directed to such questions as: "Is this the best way?" "Does this have to be done?" "How else can this be used?"

How do you get ideas? Here are five ways to go about it:

1. Make up your mind that you can come up with ideas the same as anybody else. Be unsatisfied with yourself until you do. Get started.

2. Increase your knowledge by studying. Do things you haven't tried before. Develop your imagination.

3. Participate in discussions. Listen to people and learn about their problems. Get around.

4. Plan your work and whatever else you intend to do. Get in the habit of thinking. Organize yourself and your efforts.

5. Learn from your mistakes. Shun discouragement. Always be willing to try again.

You can get an idea anytime because your subconscious mind is continually working. To avoid losing an idea, carry a small notebook with you at all times, and get in the habit of writing down ideas so that you don't forget them. While not every idea you will record will be successful or immediately useful, you will find that some are just what you need later.

—— 6 ——

How to Motivate Others to Work with You

How to Connect Motivation to People's Needs

People at all levels must feel that they are needed. If you can get across to a man that his company needs him and that the work he does is important, then you can motivate him.

What are people's needs? One strong need is to feel "in" on things. Safety Manger Dan Anderson was expected to issue Operating Procedures for various jobs in his manufacturing plant. But since he was a staff man, he was not always well-informed on the line operations and functions of the Production Department.

Dan's boss realized that Dan needed to keep well-informed, so he put Dan on the "mailing list" for managerial reports, memos, and letters. This not only gave Dan needed information, but also provided him with an ego-satisfier which motivated him to do a better, more thorough job.

When a man feels that he is recognized as a member of the group he is more inclined to contribute to that group's efforts.

How Keeping People Informed Pays Off

If a leader sees to it that his people share in "his" plans, then those plans become "theirs," too. W. W. McCullough, Production Superintendent at a Goodyear Tire and Rubber Company plant, realized that his supervisors on the night shifts often were faced with problems in scheduling and product flow priority. He made an effort to continually keep them informed on these matters with notes in the plant log book. McCullough also had a keen sense of insight which enabled him to anticipate difficulties. His suggested solutions were there in writing for the men to read. The supervisors responded with notes of their own on trends, unusual events, and equipment malfunctions.

The man who keeps his people informed is, in turn, kept informed. All, including the company, benefit.

The Ego Need

Knowing that our accomplishments may be noticed or recognized later, each of us wants to be able to say, "*I* did that part of the job"; "*I* was responsible for seeing that this job was done"; "*That* was my work."

Two Important Needs

In today's world, satisfaction with their work is probably people's most important need. How does a man gain satisfaction from his work? By being able to participate in setting the job's content and the way in which it's done, by having certain responsibilities, and by chances to obtain promotions.

A man needs to be able to *grow* on the job. Growth is achieved when the job has a challenge, when it demands attention, when it is interesting.

How do you enable a man to grow on the job? In a large industrial plant, pipefitter supervisor Jack Whitman uses this method: when Jack gets a new work order to install a system, he has a sketch made of the general layout, giving only the major piping details such as direction, line size, and type of material. Then he hands it to the pipefitters with the remark: "See me if you have any questions."

The pipefitters have a challenge requiring their skill and knowledge in the matters of valving, by-passes, gauges, strainers, unions, and the like which should be put into the system. This makes the work interesting. Moreover, they are rightfully proud when they see the finished job in operation. They tackle the next job willingly and with more experience.

Try this approach tomorrow when you ask somebody to do something for you by leaving some of the details unanswered. You'll get a more satisfied worker and perhaps a better job.

Another Important Need

Praise is another need. Everyone needs to occasionally hear that he or she has done a good job. Praise arouses feelings of competence and ability which, in turn, motivates or leads to future display of those skills.

Two unfortunate things happen when we fail to give praise. First, we risk that the one deserving of praise will not continue to do a good job for lack of encouragement. Second, we don't take advantage of the chance to reward someone, which is always a pleasant job. In both instances the opportunity to provide motivation for the future is missed.

What Praise Does

At an informal gathering, "Slim" Breeding was being recognized for 25 years of faithful service to his company. Much praise was being lavished in his direction in the presence of his peers. Without taking away any of what was due "Slim," Ron Davis, the department manager, saw an opportunity to motivate a fellow worker, Joe Ford.

"You know, Slim, in all those years I've never seen you have a serious disagreement with anybody—a remarkable thing with all the pressures you fellows have to work under," Davis said. "Joe, you, too, have this knack of getting along with everybody. I wish I could say the same for myself."

While few people remembered that Joe Ford's name was mentioned at this ceremony, Joe did. He may not have recognized the motivational "push," but he remembered the speech, as he later confided to the manager. It also showed in his willingness to volunteer for distasteful jobs during the next few months.

How to Use Pride to Motivate

You can motivate your people by appealing to their pride, another of their needs. Mention of an achievement, a deed that a person has a right to be proud of, gives him an emotional lift and a feeling of importance. This feeling leads to motivation by spurring him to act in the same manner, show his capabilities, and live up to his fine reputation.

When you appeal to a person's pride you must be sincere. Your method of complimenting must be honest. You give a dishonest compliment when you exaggerate the worth or value of a deed, or when you have your facts wrong while professing to be very knowledgeable. An honest compliment rings true. It is expressed simply, to the point, and without emotion.

How Understanding Motivates People

Motivation is accomplished when a man knows that he is understood, when his thinking is accepted. It pleases him emotionally.

A worker needs to protect his self-esteem. He does not want to have to defend himself. Each person has an ego that says he is worthwhile and that what he does is important. It may not always show, but it is there.

What Needs to Look for

To effectively handle someone's needs, look for those needs that go along with those of the company or group. When needs are common, a worker as well as his company benefit when they are satisfied.

As almost everyone's physical and cultural needs are usually satisfied today, such needs are not motivators for them. We must look for their psychological needs.

The Relation of Effort to Needs

You should be sure that each of your people knows that extra efforts on the job are rewarded. Calling attention to the fact that doing a bit more will be appreciated and rewarded may be all that one of your workers needs to hear to make him do that better job or turn out more work.

All that you need to do to motivate somebody else may be to ask him to do something for you.

Five Basic Rules for Getting Things Done Through Others

One of the major problems of the business world today is motivation of people to do their jobs willingly and efficiently. How do you get someone to want to do a better, more effective job? What does it take to make people like their jobs? Here are five rules for getting things done through others:

Rule 1. Learn What Your People Want from Their Jobs.

If you wish to know why people behave as they do, look into each individual's background and accomplishments. Knowing someone's likes and dislikes will help you in motivating him.

One man (or woman) takes special pride in working quickly. Another is more interested in thoroughness. One person prefers to work mostly by himself. Another person is more of a "team member." Get to know each worker in your group.

Manager Jim Wilson talked with Tom Goodman, a new electrical engineer, and found out Tom was an expert in circuit design and trouble-shooting. Jim learned that Tom loved to solve problems involving electrical failure. It wasn't unusual, Jim noticed, to find Tom in the plant after-hours, working until he had solved a problem, even though he had already provided a temporary remedy to avoid production downtime. His manager responded by granting Tom an afternoon off occasionally.

Rule 2. Give People Credit for Good Work.

Recognition is more important to many people than are salary or working conditions. People want to be given credit for their work.

Safety and good housekeeping awards can do this in the factory. A good way to handle this is to make the award when most of the group is together, such as at a coffee break or during the lunch hour.

The posting of newspaper clippings on the company bulletin board also informs employees of deeds and feats of their fellow workers. Suggestion awards given out in group gatherings often accomplish more in motivating people than the money itself does.

Tell someone when he has done a good job and when he has done more than was asked of him. Everyone likes sincere praise.

People doing similar jobs like to be treated equally; they dislike favoritism. The effective manager or supervisor "spreads" his dirty jobs, as well as his clean assignments, so that all of his people get their share of each.

Rule 3. Communicate with Your People.

People look for pleasant environments and friendly conversation with others, regardless of job level. They appreciate friendly remarks by their superiors.

You can inspire your people by talking with them. Many times a man may lack motivation simply because he does not know how he fits in the group, what part he will play. Tell each individual what you expect of him on the job and how he will benefit from what is going to be done.

Most people like to "know the score," to know what is going on, even if they are not directly involved. They have a team spirit in this respect.

Communicating involves more than just talking to people; it is a two-way process. You must also *listen* when they talk to you. Observation alone is not enough for full understanding. When talks take place between a man and his boss, both must be interested in learning.

Rule 4. Show Enthusiasm.

Show that you are excited about working on various projects or jobs. If you can let your people see that you are eager and anxious to get each job done, they will tend to be that way, also.

Are you optimistic in your outlook? Do you feel and show that the goals you have set can be accomplished? A good attitude simplifies the motivating of other people.

Enthusiasm can be catching. Be positive in your statements and actions. The will to win is often the only difference between the winner and the loser.

Rule 5. Set Goals for Your People.

A leader sets goals for his people and then helps them to achieve those goals. His help includes providing opportunities, recognizing obstacles, and working towards opening clearer paths to getting things done.

Many organizations have found that management by objectives clarifies job responsibilities and goals. Bill Schmitz, Eastern division sales manager of a large industrial products company, sits down with his salesmen each year to map out the volume of business expected from each man. Individual accounts are discussed and promotions for each product line are organized. Bill's setting of definite goals helps his men when they are in the field on their own.

You can lead people by being a model for them. Arouse an individual to pattern his behavior after yours. Do this by performing your job in an exciting, active manner.

A manager has the opportunity to show his enthusiasm if he is near his people and they can see how he handles his own work. Even when his workers cannot often see him at work, they will respond to a hearty, vigorous attitude.

By giving people a good example to follow, you motivate them to similar performance.

How to Use Motivation to Change Behavior

To get people to do things willingly they must *want* to do those things. How do you get them to want to do things? By appealing to their intelligence and reason, by letting them see why a job should be done.

Jim Blackwell, chemical engineer on his way up to be a technical superintendent, appreciated the training he received in the laboratory because his superior, Russ Baldwin, explained *why* he was doing certain experiments and gave the reasons *why* they were done in a certain manner. For example, Russ explained that a standard procedure is followed so that, regardless of who ran the tests, no other variables would be introduced.

Trying to force someone to do something when he cannot see how he will benefit is sometimes difficult to do. He may do the job, but his heart will not be in it, and the quality of his work may be poor as a result.

How a Reward Helps

Picture the son who is asked to wash the family car with no reward. But give him the opportunity of using the car that evening on a date and note the different job that results.

There are many ways in which rewards for creativity, productivity, and dedication can be given to employees, and perhaps there should be more. Suggestion awards are probably the most common. However, recently some new ideas have been tried: a day off with pay is awarded by a few companies for an unbroken attendance record; redemption stamps are offered for perfect safety records; patents are issued in the individual's name. But whatever the reward, it should be of sufficient value to make it worthwhile to employees. They should experience pride in receiving it.

Praise Is Better Than Criticism

Bob Johnsen, a young mechanic, was having trouble getting along with his fellow workmen and his supervisors. He didn't seem interested in the job. He frequently left the man with whom he was working to wander around the plant, take an unscheduled coffee break, or make a phone call. Although his foreman docked his pay for one-half hour one day, his behavior did not change.

One morning an important maintenance job came up. A close-clearance, critical machine had broken down. Bob's supervisor, John Hansen, saw the opportunity to help him as well as help the company.

Bob was called to the office where John told him that the maintenance department needed to put its best man on the repair since careful work was required. John said that he knew that Bob could do the job better and faster than any man the company had. Bob was asked if he wanted the job.

Bob jumped at the chance and did an excellent job. Today he no longer is shunned by his fellow workers and he has improved on productivity. He responded when praise was offered rather than criticism. This approach on the part of his supervisor motivated him and was the basic reason for his change in behavior.

How to Use Appreciation to Motivate

Here are three principles that apply to how people think and feel about other people.

We usually like people who make an effort in our behalf.

Harry Viergutz, chief chemist for The Milwaukee Road, went out of his way each summer to help the young chemists who were working part-time for the railroad. His advice and counseling helped to prepare them for industrial jobs when they finished school. They liked Harry and were grateful to him because they knew he was doing more than he needed to—there were not many openings for jobs as chemists with the railroad.

When we express our appreciation we motivate people to continue helping us and others.

We think well of people that recognize our importance by their actions or awareness.

Albert (Bud) Jones, district manager for Toledo Scale Company in the Midwest, makes a point of sending personal congratulations to his customers and business acquaintances whenever he hears of promotions, transfers, or special accomplishments. This not only strengthens friendships, but undoubtedly also helps his business.

You can use this axiom to motivate someone, be liked, and get a job done at the same time. You can show the other fellow that you are aware of his responsibilities and the job he is doing. By your actions you can let him know that you feel he is important.

People that like the same things usually like each other.

Have you noticed that the best friends of people are those who belong to the same club, like the same sports, or do the same type of work? People interested in performing their jobs in the same manner usually get along well together. This is a good thing to remember when two men must be assigned to a job. Two men who both do careful, meticulous work will get along better with each other than will one who is careful and one who is careless. Consider this the next time you have a job to be done which requires extraordinary attention.

The Value of Appreciation

You can see the value of appreciation if you tell one of your people that you have confidence in him, that you know he can produce, and that you are willing to give him a chance. By saying that you appreciate what he has done in the past, you motivate him to respond with more of the same.

In talking with someone, mention it when he has achieved something noteworthy. Periodically let him know what good work means to you. For example, say, "I appreciate the extra time you put on the job yesterday. You really got us out of a spot. Thanks."

Appreciation is sometimes shown by a financial reward. My son, John, gave Cameron Webber, our guide on a fishing trip, a very liberal tip after his first day with us. We had done very well with his help, landing some unusually large pike. The next day we requested he lead us in some pickerel fishing, a type which up to that day had been very unfruitful, according to the fishing lodge manager.

Cameron took us to a distant lake, showed us the tackle and technique. We "limited out" with 16 beauties before lunch, and Cameron earned himself a lot of praise and another tip.

Motivation is similar to learning in that the individual who responds must be willing to be motivated. He is more likely to be willing if he thinks that what he does will be appreciated; and if he is told that what he has done in the past was appreciated, it is easier for him to continue to do a good job.

Appreciation can also be shown through public recognition by news media. It carries an impact, particularly when attention is called to the fact that the job was done under unfavorable conditions such as time, location, or weather. Call the editor of your company publication or the local newspaper when you have some interesting accomplishment of one of your people to report.

How to Use Psychology to Motivate

Many people are naturally negative. When approached with a proposition they are suspicious and doubtful. "What does this fellow want? What will I have to do? Will it cost me money or time?"

Dr. Howard Bern wanted a subject for a hypnotism demonstration he was going to give at the home of one of his patients in a group presentation. The request was made to Mike Murphy, a medical student at the University of Chicago. Mike was a bit fearful at first. Dr. Bern pointed out that the experience of being hypnotized to a person studying in the field of medicine was something that would be quite valuable and not readily available to everyone. When Mike realized this, he agreed to be hypnotized. Dr. Bern showed Mike the worth of the opportunity to himself.

How to Gain Cooperation

How do you overcome someone's apprehension to your proposal? One answer is to show early in your conversation what's in it for him—how he will benefit—what he can gain.

His thinking then will be positive and be concerned with himself rather than with you. How *you* might gain will be secondary to how *he* will be better off.

Try this philosophy the next time you need someone's cooperation. Be sure that he sees what he will get out of it.

Getting a Lift Psychologically

You can motivate somebody by showing him how to give himself a lift. You can show him how he can change his habits in many ways, even if only temporarily, and gain from so doing. Here are ways to go about getting a lift.

Change Clothes.

Undoubtedly each of us has a favorite suit—we like it because of its particular weave, color, or design. Our general feeling is better when we're wearing that suit. When we feel the need for a mental lift we should wear it and gain the benefit.

If someone tells you that he has no special item of clothing that can do this for him, suggest he look for some different fabrics or colors and buy a new suit. Today's younger people are exploiting variety in dress as a way of asserting independence. You can "refresh" someone by suggesting that he change "his" style occasionally.

Often a bath or shower followed by donning clean clothes can make one feel renewed and ambitious. The water washes away tiredness and makes one feel "alive" again.

A man may have a favorite cologne or aftershave lotion that he saves for special occasions. A woman probably has a favorite perfume. They should use these when they need emotional support.

Vary Eating.

John Thompson remarked to his boss, Bill White, "I sure hate to come back to work after a vacation. It seems like every day is the same—same drive to work, same food for lunch, same problems with the work. I get tired of the same thing every day."

Bill asked him if he had had a good breakfast. Bill's own experience was that the day just didn't go right if he didn't have a good morning meal. Bill learned that John always had dry cereal for breakfast except when he was not at home, such as when visiting or traveling. After Bill's suggestion to change to food he had when he was enjoying himself, he began to look forward to breakfast and it gave him a better start on his day.

Is lunch just a snack for your workers? Why not suggest to them that they vary this pause in the day; maybe eat a full meal, or go to a new restaurant. The chance to "get away" from the office or plant at the noon hour once in a while may give them a "breather" which enables them to return to their work in a better frame of mind.

For the main meal of the day, people might consider "when," "what," "where," and "how" for a change in procedure. Dick Willard felt his family needed a supper-time change. He suggested to his wife that the family eat an hour later to build up anticipation and eliminate rush. For "what" they might try a special appetizer or an exotic main course. Taking care of the "where" is easy, even at home—another room in the house can create a touch of innovation. They might try a meal by candlelight . . . with background music . . . before the TV set . . . or using chopsticks.

Reward Oneself.

Benny Tavinello, contractor, rewarded himself after completing a tedious job. He took some time away from his work with a day's vacation to do something he especially liked, such as fishing or wood-working. When he returned to work he was rested and feeling good.

Even though you may work for someone else, you should try to "change your pace" after a grueling task has been completed. If other work has been accumulating, pick out that which requires little effort or that which is most enjoyable. In the middle of the day a small thing such as an extra cup of coffee or a snack which you usually don't buy can act as your reward by your designating it as such.

Break the montony of always looking for jobs to do around the house by giving yourself a day off once in a while to just loaf, enjoy nature, and relax.

Improving One's Outlook.

If Joe Jones, who works for you, says that his job has become too routine and all the people he works with are dull, point out to him that he's missing something.

He can find something unique in almost every person if he will look for it. One worker will have an unusual hobby, another will be an expert on a subject which seems totally unrelated to his general skill and knowledge.

As for his own job, Joe should be thinking about how it could be changed so that it would become more interesting and challenging. There's always a better way of doing things. A person must *want* to do a better job. Being friendly and cooperative with people is one way to start doing it.

Helping Others.

Dick Hogan, instrument repairman, says that the principles he
lives by are with him to aid him spiritually when the going gets rough.
Dick feels good when he helps another person and when he does a job
unusually well—everytime he does a good job he pays himself a compliment. As a result he gains recognition and rewards. Dick's faith in
himself gives him an inner satisfaction which acts as an emotional lift.

Alter Procedures.

Have you tried changing the order in which you do your daily
work? Tackle some of the shorter jobs first so that you can get job
satisfaction sooner and see some results. Also, if you can, avoid staying
with a single job until it becomes drudgery.

When Violet Browning, secretary to the Plant Manager, sees that
she needs to do some filing in addition to writing several letters, she
switches back and forth on filing and writing. An individual's "staying
power" on the job often can be extended if tasks are alternated.

You can encourage someone when you see he has a number of
similar or identical things to do. Rich Collins was asked by his wife to
refinish several pieces of furniture, a job which would take many hours
of several days. She suggested that he do one of them completely before
starting on the others. The stimulating effect of seeing a completed
beautiful object pushed him to complete the other pieces.

Look to Other People.

You can obtain hope and be cheered by other people without
actually asking for their help. A short visit with another person can do
this.

Why not have a morning cup of coffee with a neighbor or nearby
friend? Knowing that other people are interested in him may cause the
friend to offer cheerful words and worthwhile ideas. You may be
pleasantly surprised to find that visits give you a lift in getting back to
work.

John Sisty, Chief, Engineering Division of the Veterans Administration Hospital in North Carolina, is an observant man and occasionally will see an unhappy-looking worker as he tours the hospital. When he does, he makes a point of stopping for a few minutes to talk with him. He finds that he usually has the fellow in a better frame of mind when he leaves.

How to Make Yourself Felt Psychologically

You probably have seen someone who dominates a group without saying a word, who merely needs to clear his throat to get everyone's attention. How does he do it?

The answer, according to Michael Argyle of the Institute of Experimental Psychology at Oxford University, is that he "takes over" by using simple actions or mannerisms. When he speaks he uses a loud decisive voice. He holds himself very erect, looks people straight in the eye, and seldom smiles.

You, too, can make yourself felt. How? Just start by expressing your viewpoint when you're in a group discussion. Say it as if it were the *only* correct viewpoint one could possibly have in the particular situation. Your tone of voice will help. Speak with authority and you will be looked upon as the person who knows.

Just to prove to yourself that you can be a dominant person if you wish, try this:

Pick a current subject from the news and read all you can about it. Get as many facts as possible. Then, when you're with other people, bring up the subject if someone else doesn't do so. Analyze the subject for the group as you see it by stating facts and figures. You'll be in the limelight because very few people take the time to pursue a subject deeply.

Usually only strong leaders are able to perform continually in this manner. But, any confident person can, if he wishes, make himself psychologically impressive.

How to Make Others Feel Important

Each of us has an ego—"I am important and want to be respected." "Don't tell me how to live my life." "I want my viewpoint considered, too."

If we could only realize this and remember it we would always talk to the other fellow with *his viewpoint* in mind, and we would make him feel important.

When someone feels important he is motivated to prove it to the world by his actions and deeds. You can make someone feel important by instilling in him a feeling of personal worth. Tell him how good he can be, that he has the potential to go far.

To make people feel important you must let them know that they are being treated fairly and decently. If workers in a plant feel that their eating areas and restrooms are not clean and neat, they think that nobody in management cares about them. You can turn this around by providing pleasant, colorful, and well-arranged work areas to make people like their place of work and the job they do. A feeling of importance usually leads to higher quality performance.

If you don't have authority to order changes in work conditions, complain to top bosses on behalf of your workers. When they see you're trying to help, they'll show their loyalty to you.

Tom Shelby, an interior decorator, was showing a female prospective customer some lamps in a catalog. "What do you think of this one?" he asked.

"Beautiful, absolutely beautiful. I really go for that," she answered.

Tom immediately called his buyer. "Look, Mary," he said excitedly, "She likes this lamp, the one we wondered about." "Let's order one for our display room right away."

Would you agree that the prospective customer felt important after hearing those words?

How to Motivate Through Job Enrichment

Few people have the freedom to do the type of work they like the most. Many people are working on a job because they have to in order to make a living. It is difficult to motivate someone if he doesn't like his job, and it's just about impossible if he doesn't have the aptitude to do it well.

Frederick Herzberg is an advocate of job enrichment as the means of motivation. He defines job enrichment as changing the job so that it provides the opportunity for the employee's psychological growth. The term should not be confused with job enlargement which merely makes a job structurally bigger.

How do you enrich a job? You change it so that it contains motivator factors. You add motivators such as: responsibility, personal achievement, recognition, growth, learning, and advancement.

Job enrichment should not be a one-shot program but a continuous management function. You don't have to give attention to job content constantly however, since the initial changes made to a job usually last a long time.

How to Put Motivation into Jobs

You can put motivation into jobs by permitting the workers to decide for themselves how their jobs should be handled. By giving each man the opportunity to do his job the way *he* would like to do it, he will feel more responsible and thereby have a greater interest.

For example, supermarket store managers can enrich their employees' jobs by changing assignments. They can assign all the tasks of a department to one individual. In the dairy section, the man or woman in charge would order all the products from the warehouse in the quantities needed, unpack cartons, attach price tags, arrange the shelves, and handle cleaning and upkeep of shelves and utilities. In reality, he or she would run his own little dairy store handling all the details. This is job enrichment to the individual who normally would handle only one or a few of these functions.

Job Enlargement

This contrasts with job enlargement which is simply to make one person responsible for arranging shelves in the canned goods section of the store and have him also arrange shelves in cereals and paper products, in other words, give him a larger quantity of work of the same type—arranging shelves.

Dr. Robert Ford of the American Telephone and Telegraph Company recently pointed out how his company was able to get its employees to enjoy their work more and take greater pride in it. In doing so the employees were motivated to accomplish a great deal more than before their job responsibilities were changed.

In one case the girls in the Customer Service Department were permitted to write their own replies to customer and stockholder questions. Previously they had typed out letters of the form nature and signed the department manager's name. When this brought an improvement in morale and a greater amount of work accomplished, the girls were given their own stationery with their names on the letterheads. Turnover in the Customer Service Department dropped significantly, complaints were handled more efficiently, and stockholders were pleased with the personal attention they received to their questions.

Other Ways to Enrich Jobs

American Telephone and Telegraph found a way to enrich their employees' jobs in another department, too. The preparation of telephone directories involved many people in the solicitation of listings, arrangement in the book, billing, indexing, and constant and continual confirmation of numbers. With individuals assigned to each of these tasks, pride in accomplishment was difficult to realize. And, as might be expected, frequent errors and omissions were the rule in many books.

The company changed this by rearranging job scopes. Where the quantity of work for a single directory was large, individuals were given *all* the tasks involved with the listing of a single or several letters of the alphabet. More pride was realized by each person under this plan since responsibilities became much broader. The ultimate was reached by several girls when, in the case of small cities, one girl was given the authority and responsibility for the complete handling of the directory with her name on the cover stating this fact.

Although it may appear to be difficult to enrich some jobs, you should investigate and consider a job from the worker's viewpoint. Is it monotonous? Can he get pride and satisfaction from the work? Can you increase his responsibility?

You can enrich a man's job by giving him an opportunity to do some of the work normally done by his supervisor. For example, let him learn and be responsible for the financial or accounting part of the work he is doing.

The RCA Service Company in Akron, Ohio, trains the home servicemen to handle *all* the models of *all* their appliances, rather than have individuals who service only stoves or only washing machines.

The manager of the radio and television repair shop in our town has given his repairmen more responsibility and at the same time reduced his need for clerical help. His men see that the right type and number of replacement parts are ordered and on hand—they work directly with the supply house salesmen. The men also figure out their own repair bills and call the customers with estimates and when repairs have been completed. In this way the customer is given more attention since he talks with the man who did the work, and can even request that man's service on future calls.

You can more effectively handle workers when they like their work and it contains the right motivation factors.

7

How to Work with the Boss

Aside from receiving your paycheck, nothing can make a job more enjoyable than being on good terms with your boss. Having the boss pleased with you raises your enthusiasm for the job and makes it more interesting. You feel more secure and your goal of an even better job seems more attainable.

But what does it take to please the boss? What do bosses look for, expect, and sometimes demand in the way of action and performance from the people who work for them?

Some things the boss may ask of you may seem unreasonable, but most, you must agree, are only what should be expected of you in your job. If you wish to be promoted, you'll be constantly doing your best and continually making an effort to please him.

How to Learn What the Boss Wants

To be accepted by your superior, you must know what he expects of you and then deliver it. You need to learn what his bases are for judging you and how he thinks you should handle your job.

Whatever the boss wants, it's up to you to find out. If after working for him a short while you have not learned this, you should sit down with him and discuss the subject. Knowing what he expects of you will make you feel better by relieving any fear you had of not pleasing him.

Jack Larson, development manager for a large plastic fabricating company, has found that his boss was not concerned with how he solved problems or reached decisions. But the boss of Tom Reynolds, packaging manager for the same company, likes to know the details of plant problems and how Tom handles them. Bosses often wish to know the source of information, perhaps to judge if they would have looked for it there or if they consider it reliable.

The top executives of Pert & Stone, a public relations firm, like to be consulted frequently by their field representatives. Perhaps this helps to satisfy their ego in that they can feel that they are contributing their experience and knowledge in helping other people with their work.

Some bosses like to be kept fully informed, to be up-to-date on what has happened and how problems are being attacked. They feel that they are in a better position to report the status of a problem to their superiors as well as to be able to answer questions put to them.

All bosses are not likable people, and some are difficult to work for. But when you work for someone, you should really work *for* him. You were hired to help your boss. If you don't do this, you're failing to do your job.

All of us occasionally lose our zip and vitality. We can't always be charged up and ready to go. But the person who usually shows he's alive, ready to move, and confident in reaching his goal is most admired by the boss, as well as by others.

How to Support the Boss

If you have a boss, and most of us do have one type or another, you should be supporting him and doing your best to see that he gets ahead. If you can get him promoted you open the door for your own promotion. Isn't it natural then that you should be looking for ways to help him on his way?

In order to assist and support him you must first understand him. You need to learn his weaknesses and his strengths—then help him with his weaknesses. The way to learn more about him is to expand your communications, extend your discussions when you are together, and try to help him with *his* assignments. When you are doing work for him do it as he would, to the point where he could take credit for it himself.

Al Golding, area claims man for an insurance company in New York, looked for opportunities to help his superior with work that was the superior's responsibility, not his. Golding was perceptive in recognizing that his superior would be retiring in a few years, and if Golding knew the man's job, he would be in a good position to move into it. Undoubtedly, this was the major reason that Golding eventually got the job. Now Golding is using the same technique with his new superior.

Anyone who works for someone else has the right to give his opinion even though it may differ from that of his boss. Roy Boyles, assistant to the mayor of a large Southern city, speaks up when he works with the city council and mayor on knotty problems of city administration. But once a decision has been made, he agrees that each member of the city government should do his best to support that decision whether he agrees with it or not. This principle is accepted and practiced wherever people work together, whether it be team play in sports or department efforts in business.

The individual who doesn't cooperate because his way wasn't chosen is defeating only himself. Supporting other people is a way of understanding and demonstrating the need for cooperation. Nobody can truly become a good leader himself until he has learned to accept the leadership of others.

Why not approach the boss and ask how you can be of more value to him? You might offer to do work outside your normal duties, work that is his responsibility but which interests you. By doing this you will demonstrate that he has your support—he will appreciate it.

How do you get along with your fellow workers and those in other departments? Do you willingly cooperate? The success of sales ventures, product development, consumer service, and business in general seldom depend solely on the efforts of single individuals these days. Group efforts are needed. But there must be cooperation when people work together. Your boss will be grateful for your efforts in seeing that *his* department is doing its share, as this helps *him* get ahead.

How to Keep the Boss Informed

Keeping your boss informed is a major step in supporting him. How you do it shows your sincerity in really helping him. If you are conscientious, your reports will always be truthful and never slanted to make them seem favorable. Nor will you conveniently forget to tell him something that went wrong. Refraining from telling the boss the bad news along with the good puts him at a disadvantage if he is questioned by his superior. It also denies him the opportunity to start corrective action if he would want to do so. Besides, you only kid yourself—he is bound to learn the facts sooner or later, and then wonder why you didn't keep him informed.

How easy or difficult it is to keep your boss informed depends on his personality, temperament, and style of managing. Does he accept bad news much differently from good news? Does he expect much detail? Is he interested in figures or only general statements?

The leader who is not interested in details may become impatient and bored if you spend too much time on them. The best policy with someone like this is to refrain from offering facts and figures unless they are asked for.

One of the major problems subordinates have with upward communication is fear—fear that if a subordinate gives his boss bad news, the subordinate will be criticized or unjustly blamed. While the temptation may be strong to withhold information in order to avoid emotional outbursts, the best course is to give the boss the facts being as unemotional as you can yourself.

How to Help the Boss with His Decisions

Leaders appreciate their subordinates' offer of help in solving problems and making decisions. The subordinate can most easily present this help in the form of memos, reports, and talks which provide information. However, subordinates need to be careful in one respect on these matters—they should not try to do their leader's thinking for him.

Ralph Green, assistant to the president of Muller Corp., in talking about his job, says, "I offer to get facts which will help the president in his decisions. Along the same line, I may point out problems which he may not be aware of and get his thinking on how they should be approached. He lets me know if I can help on those things.''

To see how your boss is thinking on a problem, watch for his expression of a strong viewpoint at the outset. It will serve to steer you in the direction where you can come up with a solution which will not conflict with his opinion.

When attempting to solve complex or drawn out problems for your boss, you need to continually ''touch base'' to be sure your approach agrees with what his would be under the circumstances. If you fail to do this, you may sometime go ''off on a tangent'' and come up with a solution wholly unacceptable to him.

Bosses expect a degree of maturity in the actions of their subordinates. Although maturity grows with experience, the boss must at least see signs that subordinates are improving in this respect. He prefers well-thought-out answers to problems rather than quick, spur-of-the-moment replies.

Schoolboy tactics should be put aside when you're on the job. Show by your actions and deeds that you're a levelheaded, stable person. Keep your head, especially under tense situations, if you want to keep your job and advance rapidly.

How to Save the Boss Time

Do you run to the boss for many decisions—decisions that you should be making yourself? Avoid experiencing that foolish feeling of having overlooked the obvious. You can do this by thinking things out a bit more before consulting with him. Get more facts to solve your problems, but get them without bothering the boss. You can teach your people to do this, too, by periodically mentioning sources of information which they may need in the future. Point out that they are capable of digging up such facts as well as you can.

William R. Brown is a manager of a contracting firm in Houston. His company gets numerous requests to do small, various-type jobs and he is often burdened with details or decisions on simple matters concerning these jobs. Brown tries to have most of these things handled by a subordinate but still gets involved more than he likes. He says, ''To be useful to me, my subordinate must be capable of making decisions rather than be wishy-washy in thinking. He can save me a lot of time with these matters.''

Clint McGrew, production superintendent in a printing shop in Cleveland, had a similar problem. Despite years of experience, his foreman, Willie Schultz, often was overcautious in making decisions concerning many of the orders his department received. Willie's action on these problems took the form of memos to McGrew suggesting alternative courses of action and requesting a decision; in many cases, information which was needed to make a decision was lacking.

McGrew found himself spending too much time following up these memos and making decisions for his foreman. Realizing that this procedure could not continue, he began putting short answers on the memos and firing them back to the foreman. ''Do what you think is best,'' or ''Get it done the fastest way possible,'' and even ''Handle it!'' The memos soon stopped except for an occasional unusual case which McGrew didn't mind handling.

Here's another way to save your boss time. Volunteer for a job you know the boss faces, preferably before he has a chance to think about assigning it. You'll demonstrate initiative and show that you're interested in saving time. Offering to tackle something that is difficult lets the boss know that you are willing to take the tough as well as the easy assignments. It's the attitude the boss hopes you have when you're working for him.

You can save your boss time by being alert and aware of problems that are developing. By anticipating a turn of events, you can stay ''on top'' of a situation and know what to do when things don't go as planned. The individual who knows who to call for help or how to improvise can save his boss and his company time—and time is money.

How to Make a Good Impression

The boss will be pleased with you if you make a good impression on others. It's a sign that he has picked capable people for his department or has trained them to be that way. You create a positive image by being clean, neat, and well-groomed. Good dress and manners give strong impressions because they denote strength and stability.

For proof of the value of a good impression, watch a busy haberdashery. Notice the immediate attention given to the entering customer who is well-dressed, neat, and carries himself well. Even if all the salesmen are busy, one will certainly approach him and say that he will serve him as soon as he is able. Also, the man who makes a good impression will usually be given a choice table in a place of entertainment.

You can sense and get this attention yourself by being careful about your appearance. Conversely, you can turn people off by being dirty, disheveled, and unkempt when you approach them.

The individual who thinks his appearance is unimportant may be thought to feel similarly about his job and his responsibilities to other people. Would you have confidence in a new doctor if on your first visit to his office he attended you wearing a dirty shirt and worn-out pants? Would you hire a secretary who, at her interview, came dressed in formal clothes and excessive cosmetics?

Making a good impression means a lot in getting people to accept your ideas and help you with your work. It's another reason your boss likes to have people who impress others working for him.

Five Ways to Impress the Boss

In addition to making a favorable impression on others, you certainly want to impress your boss. While this may be more difficult, simply because he knows you and your capabilities better than other people do, this shouldn't deter you. Here are some suggestions on how to go about it:

1. Do something that needed to be handled a long time ago. Some problems never seem to get solved. By concentrating on one of these until you whip it, you will be noticed as an achiever.

Rick Jones was hired as a new engineer in a manufacturing plant in Ohio. One of the first jobs Rick handled was getting the thermostat relocated on an electric truck, thus solving the problem of motor kickout after a short period of operation. The motor failure had been put up with for more than a year because nobody had made a sincere effort to correct it. Rick's boss never has forgotten this incident and still admires him for it.

2. Keep busy. Almost any job has duties and responsibilities that

can be neglected. Look for them and give them your attention. After all, you are being paid to produce. If the work doesn't come to you, go out after it.

3. Learn your job from all angles. Study the language of your profession so that you'll be at ease when talking with and listening to your peers and your superiors. Knowing the terminology of your job enables you to broaden your knowledge when you associate with experts in your field.

4. Be friendly, cooperative, and anxious to please other people. Be interested in their problems and try to do things for them. You'll be respected in your job functions. Bosses other than your own hear about these things and wish you were working for them.

Bill Weber started out as a foreman in the production department of a metal fabricating plant in Milwaukee. In performing his job he became well-liked by the engineering department because of his cooperation in trying out and operating new equipment. It wasn't long before the manager of the engineering department asked that he be transferred to his department. Today Bill is the manager of that department.

5. Continually try to improve yourself in your knowledge and know-how. Participation in professional groups and attendance at seminars help to broaden your education. Books, college courses, and trade literature offer you an opportunity to know more about your job and related jobs.

Impressing the boss can't help but pay off in earning more respect, better pay, or promotion. These things are certainly worth the effort you may expend.

How to Avoid Embarrassing the Boss

A manager is sometimes embarrassed when he is asked a question by his superior that he cannot answer because his subordinates have not kept him informed. His people could save him this embarrassment if they would make more of an effort to keep him up-to-date on matters about which he should know.

S. L. Worden, plant manager in a manufacturing company in New

Jersey, says, "A leader needs upward communication from his people if he is to make effective decisions. I make a point of talking with my department managers several times a day to keep informed, but often I must struggle to learn what they are doing because few people offer to tell me."

Your boss will appreciate your keeping him informed. Give him the bad news along with the good. Eventually he will learn both anyway, and if you've suppressed the bad, you may be asked to explain why.

Saying something you shouldn't is another way by which you might embarrass your boss. "Pop" Heller, section head for Close Company in New York, says, "A fellow has to be careful of what he says when talking with the boss' boss. For example, there's always a question of how much my boss has claimed on how far along we are on new product lines. He tends to exaggerate anyway, so I sometimes have to evade direct questions."

How you talk to other people might also embarrass the boss. He frowns on sarcasm and criticism from you when you express your opinions, and he may be embarrassed if you do this to others in front of him. Neither will finding fault and making fun of people gain the boss' support. A tactful individual gets his point across without hurting other people's feelings.

Your boss is probably also sensitive to criticism of his own actions. Avoid the use of his name as leverage to get things done. He should never be sorry he let you act for him.

The boss likes to feel that he can depend on you, particularly when it comes to doing good work and doing it within a certain time period. He likes to see careful work, completed on schedule, followed by concrete recommendations.

He hopes you'll never let him down and always keep your word. Can he trust and rely on you to handle his job in his absence?

How to Get the Boss to Help You

The way to get your boss to help you is to ask for that help. Who else is better qualified to discuss your problems and help you solve them? Your boss may have held your job at one time. Even if he has not, he should understand your position and know about your problems. Besides, if you do not need to ask for help once in a while, you either are not getting your job done or not doing it as well as you should.

You must be careful about one thing, however. Before approaching your boss with a problem, be sure you have done some thinking on it yourself. Otherwise you can fall into the habit of going to him with problems that you should have handled yourself.

There is always the temptation to say, "I'll have to ask the boss about this," when it's really your decision to make. Getting into such a habit also leads to a lack of confidence in you from your own subordinates. You'll know when this happens—one of your people will say to you, "Ask the boss if I can . . ." or "Here's something to check with the boss on. . . ."

Be frank and honest when asking the boss to help you. You should not feel guilty about taking his time with your problems; they are his problems, too, for you are part of his organization.

How Improving Yourself Pleases the Boss

The boss depends on you and his other people to help him in making plans and decisions. The more knowledgeable you are, the more training you've had, and the more efficiently you work, the more valuable and helpful you can be to him.

Continuing your education is the best way you can improve yourself. Most people stop their formal learning when they get out of school. It stands to reason that the longer they've been out, the less educated they are, comparatively speaking. Why? Because the people who continue their education surpass them in having a broader viewpoint and in being aware of better work methods.

The world is continually changing in the way jobs are being done and in the facilities and equipment provided to do them. People's attitudes and ways of thinking also are changing. The man who has a college education or its equivalent is generally better equipped to make decisions and to lead people than the man who has gone no further than high school. And the man who continues his studies and keeps up-to-date is more likely to go further in his company than the man who doesn't care.

Earl Nightingale, Chairman of the Board of his corporation, Nightingale-Conant Corp. of Chicago, believes that managers can solve problems, such as declining productivity and rising costs, by more creative thinking. But most people don't do any more than they have to between crises. Nightingale feels that nearly every business problem is a problem involving people and nearly every business advance will spring from a better understanding of human resources and ways of tapping them.

Are you continually trying to improve yourself? There's a lot to be gained, aside from obviously pleasing your boss. Personal satisfaction, more recognition, a better job, and a higher standard of living are a few of the benefits you can reap from your efforts.

How Bosses Should Treat Their People

When working for someone you try to do your best to please him. You know from experience that if he is happy with your work, your chance of getting an increase in pay or a promotion are better than if you just do a mediocre job. Also, having the boss pleased with you makes your work enjoyable and worthwhile.

But how do you want your boss to treat you? What would you like to have your boss do to make your job more pleasant and more in line with your abilities?

The Dartnell Institute of Management surveyed a group of secretaries on what they wanted their bosses to do to make their jobs more challenging and more in keeping with their skills. Here are the answers the Institute received:

1. Tell me what he expects.

2. Spend less time giving instructions and let me solve problems by myself.

3. Listen to my suggestions.

4. Broaden his views on women's capabilities.

5. Verbally show appreciation.

6. Give me background information on company problems.

7. Plan his work schedule better for my benefit.

8. Plan farther ahead for major projects.

9. Not retract authority once it is given.

10. When assigning a job, give me the authority necessary to assure its completion.

11. Inform me of his itinerary, meetings, and appointments.

12. Stop talking down to me.

13. Be more consistent in controlling his work procedures.

14. Set a better example regarding adherence to company policy.

15. Let me set up my own systems, within reason.

16. Let me know what promotions are available to me beyond the secretarial level.

17. Realize that I have no control over airline schedules.

Judging from these answers, bosses exert a great influence on the motivation and performance of their subordinates. How do you treat your people? Maybe you need to look to your own actions if your people do not please you as much as you think they should.

How You Can Improve Your Job

In addition to the many ways already mentioned that you can please your boss, simply doing a better job will obviously make your boss happy. What does doing a better job involve? The secretaries surveyed by the Dartnell Institute of Management offered these answers:

1. Do more business reading, continue my education, and increase my knowledge of the company.

2. Further develop my verbal skills.

3. Offer more suggestions.

4. Let my boss know what responsibilities I want and can assume.

5. Learn more about my boss' personality and work responsibilities.

6. Be more conscious of the time I waste.

Most effective managers, says Robert M. Shornick, President, RMS Associates, St. Louis, "would rather have women with a lot of initiative—women they have to slow down sometimes, rather than women they have to prod.''

Many bosses would like their secretaries to take more independent action than the secretaries think they should. Mr. Shornick feels that the key to the whole matter of transforming a secretary into a management assistant is "a good rapport between the secretary and her manager—a full understanding between them of his specific goals—what he's trying to accomplish for himself, his department, and his company.''

How to Become Indispensable

Want the boss to feel that you are indispensable? While you may say that's a big order, your boss can be influenced to think in this direction if you start doing things to justify such thoughts. Here are the ways you can get and deserve such a rating:

1. Always be ready to volunteer for an assignment regardless of how distasteful it might be. If the boss knows that he has someone willing to tackle any job the minute it's mentioned, he can be more aggressive with his superior in planning and carrying out projects desired by the company.

2. Develop your skills to the point where you can handle the job of anyone now working for your boss. Think what this can mean to the boss in the way of assurance that any particular job can be handled on any specific day.

3. Continually be looking for problems to solve—and establish a high success percentage in handling them. Look for and accept more responsibility. Search out trouble and correct it.

4. Keep improving yourself by broadening your knowledge, learning new skills, and bettering your performance. Grow by studying and investigating.

5. Become an expert in your field to the point where people come to you for advice and training. Be willing and available to help anyone. Be "the authority" and get a good reputation.

If you had someone working for you who had most of these qualifications, you'd probably label him as indispensable. Why not start a self-improvement program to work towards this end? There's probably nothing else you could do to please the boss more.

How to Criticize the Boss

Touchy situation? Yes, but if approached properly, much good can come of it.

First, you must realize that nobody likes to be negatively criticized. You must be able to do so without offending and in a manner which *you* would accept if *you* were being criticized by *your* subordinate. Your boss should be made to feel that you are trying to help him. If you do it properly, he will not be hurt nor feel that you are overstepping your bounds.

Second, look upon the criticism as being justified in that what the boss is doing or not doing is hurting him through you, and get him to see it that way. If, for example, the boss is not giving you all the facts you need to effectively work on a problem, this should be pointed out to him. He will not get the problem solved as fast or as acceptably because of his failure.

While criticizing the boss should by no means be a frequent occurrence on your part (if you wish to continue working for him), an occasional incident may work to your advantage. You demonstrate that you are alert and trying to stay on top of your work. You also show that you are concerned with doing what is right for your company. Above all, you indicate that you want to do the job he would like you to do.

How to Handle Concern Over Credit

Young managers or newly-appointed leaders may sometimes be concerned that they will not get credit for their ideas and what they accomplish. They may feel that they are not noticed for the job they're doing. They may even suspect that their boss takes credit for some of their work. Such fears are almost always unfounded.

Knowledge of who was responsible for a good idea and who implemented it gets around. Besides, and more important, the better you can make your boss look to his superiors, the more appreciative your boss will be of you. Your success on the job is measured by the boss' success. If your work gets him promoted, you are in line to be moved up yourself.

Dick Willard, development manager in the electronics division of a large electrical manufacturing company, knew he was doing a good job because he and his people had come up with some new designs on controls which his company was now selling. But he wondered whether his work was being recognized. He got his answer one day when two of the top executives unexpectedly stopped in his department to compliment him and discuss progress on a new device on which he was working—and which he thought was secret.

Nobody should worry about getting credit for work well done. It will come of its own accord.

8

How to Change Indifference into Enthusiastic Performance

The desire of every leader is to have people who are enthusiastic and willing to work. Management is continually looking for such people. As for employees already on the job, keeping them alert and productive is one of the never ending problems of every leader. The leader who relaxes his efforts to create and maintain good employee attitudes leaves himself open for the takeover of poor habits.

Keeping your people enthusiastic may require the utmost of your human relations skills, but the job need not be so tough if you follow the right procedures. Once you know the extent of your task and build up momentum in your efforts, you'll find that keeping employees enthusiastic is easier when you maintain *your own* enthusiasm.

What can you do to change someone who has become indifferent? Here's how to go about it.

How to Communicate Enthusiasm

Leaders should know several ways in which they can arouse someone to become interested in his job and his company. One way is to let a subordinate "originate" his way of solving a problem. Bring up the problem and subtly suggest how to go about finding an answer, but let

145

him propose the solution. Then question it and eventually be persuaded that "his" solution is good. You can be assured that he will be enthusiastic in handling the problem to a successful conclusion.

Bob Lewis, Research Director at Post Institute, uses this technique in working with his section heads. He says he "never gives a concrete, specific assignment," but "tries to steer the fellow in the general direction" only. Lewis finds that this approach results in innovations and enthusiasm for the task which would not materialize if he told someone specifically what to do.

Some people are hard to convince to your way of thinking. The harder you try, the more skeptical they become and the more difficult it is to get them to listen and accept your ideas. Frequently, a low pressure, humorous approach has the best chance of getting people interested.

Charley White, foreman in a meatpacking company in Cleveland, has enjoyed much success with this approach. According to his boss, Jess Dile, Charley does so by being cheerful and "alive" when he gives his men assignments. Dile also says that Charley does a lot of kidding, too, when someone is slow to start or begins to "dog" it during the day. "His type of enthusiasm takes the dullness out of the work and keeps people on their toes."

Aside from personal contacts, management can use other communication means to keep employees concerned and interested with their work. Posters on the plant or office bulletin board attract attention and are a big help in getting people to think constructively. To be most effective, posters should be colorful, with short messages which are to the point. Motivation experts recommend that you use those which are slanted toward a particular problem that the company may have rather than be general in nature. For example, if your company is experiencing many eye injuries, the poster messages should stress the value of wearing safety glasses or other means of eye protection. Some industrial companies periodically run sales of safety equipment to promote safety in the plant.

Films, a company newspaper, and periodic talks by management people to the employees are other ways to get people interested in their company and to communicate enthusiasm about their work.

The giving of rewards or tokens of appreciation is a good way to promote enthusiasm in an effort. The early grade school teacher does this by giving paper stars to the children when they do well on a test or assignment. High schools and colleges award their athletes "letters" for their jackets and sweaters. Professional football players have insignias displayed on their helmets. Industry and business promote enthusiasm in company projects through letters of commendation, plaques, and mention in company publications. For example, the Goodyear Tire and Rubber Company awards gifts of increasing value to blood donors as they pass gallon contribution levels.

How to Combat Boredom

Lack of enthusiasm on the job is often blamed on boredom and uninteresting work. Leaders often have to fight a constant war on monotony to get the work out day after day. To make matters worse, a dull routine is not only the cause of inefficiency, but is also a threat to safety. The problem is particularly acute in assembly line operations where workers may repeat the same short job, hour after hour. Job enrichment is one approach to eliminating boredom; personnel people realize that ways must be found to make factory jobs more interesting and satisfying.

Medical records show that people who have strong interests and are continually busy live a longer and healthier life. Doctors report that when many of their patients complain of being tired or fatigued, they usually are not experiencing a physical ailment. Boredom is behind such feeling.

Boredom takes over when we lack interest in what we're doing. In contrast, give us something to do which we consider exciting or stimulating and we become so interested that we may lose track of time, forget to eat, and not notice that we are tiring ourselves until we finish a job. Scientists, artists, and writers, for example, may get so absorbed in their work that they are completely oblivious of other people or any time schedule.

How do you combat boredom with your people? If you can vary the type of work they do or can occasionally introduce something new, you can reduce the monotony of the work and they will become less weary. For instance, switching workers to different jobs will often make the work seem less tedious.

Win Dermody, General Manager, Military Packaging Co. of Florida, thinks that boredom on the job results more from the attitude of workers than from problems inherent in jobs. He says that people expect a job to provide more than just money to buy the necessities of life. Some people want more satisfaction from a job than management is able to put in it. Best answer to this is to try to make every worker feel his worth. An occasional comment from a boss on what a worker did and how it enabled the company to get a job handled can make the individual feel that he and his job are important.

If you can introduce competition between groups or individuals you have an opportunity to reduce boredom and, at the same time, possibly raise quality or quantity of work output. But be careful how you present such a program. Make sure you're introducing friendly rivalry with the "game" spirit behind it. The benefit to the company should not be stressed or you may not get participation.

Five Ways You Can Beat Boredom

Do you frequently become bored with your job or your life pattern? Here are five ways to stave off that feeling:

1. Look for better ways of doing your job. Putting your mind to work in such a search adds something to the job and makes you forget habit and routine. A bonus is that ideas on how problems can be solved pays off in more pleasant and easier work. The searching, inquisitive mind finds life interesting and anything but boring because there is always something new to look for, some question to be answered, and some gratification to be achieved.

2. Aim at doing a better job by either doing something faster or doing more. Give yourself some goals to shoot for, making some of them short-range so that you can realize satisfaction quickly. Consider other, more distant goals. You can build up a sense of ease if you think out what you want and expect in the future. Planning on how you can get ahead in your work and following through with action is a rewarding way of keeping your mind healthy and active.

3. Vary your schedule and your way of doing things. For exam-

ple, try doing some of your afternoon tasks in the morning and vice versa. Change by itself can make what you do more interesting, and surprisingly, may reveal better, faster, and easier ways of getting things done. A positive attitude helps to combat boredom. So does being optimistic and cheerful.

4. Start a hobby. If you already have one, try a new one. Look around for ways to make some extra money. Finding a new interest which is also profitable can be doubly rewarding. Having a hobby gives you something to look forward to when you leave your work.

5. Join some organizations. Being with people and helping others can bring much satisfaction while keeping you busy. Many people need help in this world and there are not enough people who donate time for such worthwhile causes.

How to Interest People in Their Company

All employers would like to have their employees interested in the company. People who show an interest in their jobs and what their company is doing are better workers. They have better attendance records, they are less careless, they waste less, and they promote the company with their relatives and friends. Through these things they help their company to grow and prosper.

Arousing employee interest in the company is not an easy task since they must see some benefit from it. What to say and how to say it require careful thought, a knowledge of human nature, and an ability to be convincing. Among the ways of telling people about their company are person-to-person talks, a company newspaper, notices on the bulletin boards, information leaflets handed out in pay envelopes, and department meetings.

Management needs to know if it is getting through with its messages and which media are most effective. Workers "don't want to play games," says Dr. Gordon L. Lippitt, Professor of Behavior Science, George Washington University, Washington D.C., and therefore, companies should be more direct in communicating with plant employees. "They see through management games right away, and they would rather have you lay it on the line."

Getting feedback on communications should be part of a company's program, according to Dr. Hideya Kumata, director of the International Communication Institute at Michigan State University, East Lansing, Michigan. Dr. Kumata feels that subordinates can be trained to keep in touch with their closest opinion leaders and certain key people to encourage feedback.

The average worker has misconceptions about how his company is doing profitwise and what is considered a fair amount of profit. A large rubber company surveyed its employees on how much money they thought their company was making and what they thought should be a satisfactory figure. Management was shocked to learn that many of the workers believed that the company was making a profit of 25 to 30 cents on every dollar of sales; they felt that 10 to 12 cents should be acceptable. At the time, the company was making less than 5 cents on the dollar and hadn't exceeded that figure for many years.

How to Tell About the Company

Supervisors play key roles in keeping employees informed of what's going on in their company. They owe it to their people to keep them "in the know." The supervisor who can discuss a company commercial he saw on television, or a new plant the company is building, can get his people interested in the company and create a sense of belonging.

"It is really appalling that there are millions of people who just work in a plant and feel no association with the company at all," says Walter E. Haggerty Jr., internal communications manager for Alcoa in Pittsburgh. "It is sad because they spend so much of their time at their jobs, and yet it means little more to them than a place to work. The basic problem, I think, is that they learn no economics at all in school. They tend to over-simplify things and feel that 1 cent per hour in pay doesn't amount to much. But, if in a presentation we multiply it by 2,000 working hours per year times the number of workers and come up with a big bundle of additional money which must be generated out of the plant, it starts to get through."

C. L. Stover, Plant Manager in a synthetic latex manufacturing plant, feels that interest in a company can be created if employees are told about how the company's customers use its products. Each year Stover makes a presentation to his people in the plant cafeteria several times a day so that all the employees will have an opportunity to hear him. He presents volume figures, names of customers, and end uses of the company's many types of latex. When an employee can see a company's product on the market and used by friends and relatives, he can feel some pride in saying, "*I* helped to make the latex that went on the back of that rug to make it skid-proof."

How to Build Confidence in People

The successful individual has confidence in himself. He knows he can do a certain job. He also does what he says he'll do. But how did he get that confidence? How can you give it to your people?

You can build confidence in someone in several ways. A professional develops his skill and his confidence through continual practice. Repeating, sharpening up, and trying to do a little better each time soon makes his actions almost automatic so that when the chips are down, his performance is likely to be flawless. By practicing he has built up his confidence to where he's *sure* he will do well. Examples of such confident individuals are sports figures, musicians, and artisans in many fields. If you wish to build confidence in someone, get him to practice in what he wants to be proficient.

Knowledge helps to build confidence. Knowing more than the next fellow about a job, a subject to be discussed, or how someone is likely to act under certain conditions provides an advantage when decisions must be made and action taken. The successful salesman has confidence in making a sale because he knows his product or service. He has an added edge when he knows his customer's needs, likes, and dislikes. An instructor feels confident he can teach to a greater degree when his knowledge of his subject is very broad and complete. You can make your subordinate more confident in his job by persuading him to study and learn more about it. Show confidence yourself in how you go about your own job—it will add to your credibility.

Another way you can build confidence in people is by seeing that they achieve a degree of success in what they undertake. Experience breeds confidence—when someone has once tasted success, he feels that he can repeat. Give someone an opportunity to be successful—it doesn't have to be a big achievement, but something which *through his efforts* he accomplishes a goal or realizes an ambition. His success will give him confidence in future efforts.

Using Goals to Increase Enthusiasm

Lack of enthusiasm is blamed by some people on their not seeing any advantage in being otherwise. They cannot picture a brighter future regardless of what they might do because they get no rewards or benefits from their work. They need to be shown the worth of enthusiasm.

Samuel Goldwyn said that no person who is enthusiastic about his work has anything to fear from life. All the opportunities in the world—and they are as plentiful today as ever despite what some people say—are waiting to be grasped by the people who are in love with what they are doing.

Giving people goals to shoot for is a way of getting them more interested in their job and in gaining satisfaction from their work. Most people have long-range goals which go beyond what they hope to do on the job. They may want to set aside enough money to build a new home or to send their children to college. The older workers think about their retirement. But in all cases, people's jobs are usually the means by which they can attain their goals.

Goals are important. They help us avoid discouragement and to keep moving forward. But we must occasionally get the satisfaction of actually reaching a goal. To assure this, most of our goals must be realistic and practical; we must be capable of achieving them. The sales manager who sets goals for his salesmen must be careful to not set them too high. The committee which decides how much money to go for on a charity drive must use good judgment. Being able to exceed goals also has its value in creating enthusiasm.

Some of our goals should be short-range so that we can periodically realize accomplishment. An aspiring writer should be encouraged to begin with short stories or articles rather than a book so that he will be more likely to have something published quicker and at more frequent intervals.

When you set goals for your people, start with some that are not difficult to reach, your objective being mainly to increase enthusiasm for the job. Also, solidify the success of their endeavors by making favorable comments when they achieve their goals. Everyone likes to hear that actions and accomplishments have been noticed.

The Akron, Ohio, Community Chest committee sets realistic goals for their charity drive each year. During the pledge and collection period they generate enthusiasm as well as recognize achievement through a series of Report Meetings. At these meetings free dinners are given to the area captains and division heads who are in charge of the solicitations. Percent of goal reached as well as the amount collected are announced to the group for each area. Each meeting is an occasion to acknowledge accomplishment to the moment and to generate further enthusiasm to reach 100 percent of the goal.

How to Use Flattery to Promote Enthusiasm

The world needs more flattery. If people received more compliments on what they've done and are doing, they would be more enthusiastic about their work. Flattery does some good even when it is tainted with insincerity because we all have a vain streak in us. We like to be noticed—we enjoy hearing that we've done something well —despite the fact that sometimes in our own mind we know it was not that good.

The suit salesman says you look sharp in the new suit you're thinking of buying. Of course, he says that to every prospective customer, but you accept his compliment as sincere and begin to like the suit more yourself. The teacher praises a pupil when he or she learns something, saying that not everybody would do as well, even though the pupil may be a slow learner.

Most users of flattery, however, are unaware that they are not getting the most from its use. For flattery to be most effective, it should be directed to someone's weakness, not his strength. This is where most of us fall down in its use. We will compliment a secretary for getting out a perfect letter very quickly. What she needs and would appreciate more is a compliment on how she is dressed or how she has fixed her hair. Complimenting an accountant on "breaking a hundred" on his golf game will do more for him than noticing and remarking about how his ledger books are up-to-date.

If you wish to use flattery to promote enthusiasm, look for a way to compliment someone on his accomplishment in a field in which he feels inferior or inadequate. The pride you develop will carry over into his regular job and into areas in which he is already known and expected to be good. Why don't you try this with one of your people? You'll probably surprise him, but he may also surprise you with his increased enthusiasm.

How to Get People to Communicate

Getting your people to communicate is often a big problem. If they're getting along all right they see no need to talk about it or pass information. If they are having a problem they may prefer to suffer in silence, thinking that it is not serious enough to complain about or that nothing can be done about it. What they are unaware of is that communicating can create enthusiasm and makes getting along with people easier. You realize, of course, that if you wish people to accept your ideas, you must do a good job of communicating. You must also be a good listener.

The art of listening is the key to effective communication says Professor Dominic LaRusso, University of Oregon. He feels that the important thing is not what is said, but what is heard. By listening to someone *before* you try to get him to agree with you, you'll learn what it is that may prevent him from accepting your ideas. Then you can make the proper approach to change his thinking.

A strong human need is that to belong, to be a member, and to contribute to a group. This need is satisfied through relations with other people, relations in which viewpoints are expressed and information is passed. People like to be "in" on things. You can help them by keeping them informed.

You can push people into communicating by being interested in them and their work. Ask them questions. Be friendly. It is difficult for someone to remain silent if he sees that other people are interested in him.

The job of improving communications in an organization lies

mainly between supervisor and foreman, and between foreman and the worker. People who work together face-to-face have greater problems of good communications than large groups have with each other or than top management has with workers.

Communication depends on understanding. Dr. Harry Sullivan, in his *Conceptions of Modern Psychiatry,* says, "In dealing with students, with patients, or with any group or nation the first step is to see the world through their eyes, to enter into what they are trying to do, however strange their behavior seems. Genuine communication is impossible on any other basis."

Give your people a chance to communicate by trying to understand their problems and by being a willing listener when they want to talk to you. The normally enthusiastic individual who suddenly becomes silent and seems to have lost interest in what he is doing may need a chance to "unload" his feelings. After he does so he probably will return to normal. At least he will feel better.

Three Steps to Handle an Enthusiasm Problem

You can get someone to be more enthusiastic if you do a careful job of studying his problem, followed by encouraging him and showing a friendly willingness to assist him. Here is how to go about it:

First, learn as much as you can about a problem or situation which is bothering him. Determine why it is a problem and why a simple or ready solution is not possible. Study possible answers and what they would lead to.

Second, try to understand the position of the individual who has the problem. Why does he feel as he does? Has he given any suggestion or indication of what it would take to have him change his mind? Decide your best approach to make him think and reason. Look for a way to encourage him.

Third, discuss the problem with the individual. Suggest your answer to the problem and point out its benefits, without saying anything about benefits to others. An individual lacking enthusiasm frequently doesn't care what other people think or how he affects them. Use your best argument first if you sense opposition or lack of interest.

Leaders can be more effective in maintaining enthusiasm in their people if they develop their persuasion abilities. Tom Hill, general superintendent for a road construction company, is adept at getting his engineers and laborers to work together because he works closely with them. He anticipates project difficulties and where problems may arise. At these times he pitches in himself to demonstrate how to proceed. His skill at persuasion keeps his company's contracts moving and men on the job, a necessity for meeting schedules in his line of work.

The key to raising enthusiasm in someone is being available and ready to help him, and letting him know it. Try unlocking one of your indifferent people tomorrow.

How to Make People Feel They Belong

Most people want to be aware of what's going on, whether they are directly affected or not. By keeping someone informed, you can make him feel he's part of an important group rather than just another employee; and you'll get more from him by doing this.

Raymond A. Catalano, commercial products production chief, United Nuclear Corp., New Haven, Connecticut, understands the people who work for him. He knows that each one of his people has to feel he is contributing something important, regardless of how small it might be. Catalano makes his men feel wanted by personally greeting each individual every morning, thereby assuring them that he sees them as human beings, not just workers on the job.

You can make people feel they belong by showing interest in the work they are doing and by keeping them up-to-date about jobs they will be handling next. People feel more important if they have the opportunity to say how they would like to handle a job and what should be done. You give them this opportunity when you talk about work coming up.

Another way to create interest and enthusiasm is to ask for someone's advice on how a job should be done, accepting that advice, and agreeing that the suggested procedure was a fine idea. Clever wives use this psychology to get their husbands more interested in the appearance of their home and in getting repair work done.

Telling people what their organization is doing and what problems are being encountered also helps to make people feel important. Direct mail which reports what individual members have accomplished and what people have volunteered to do helps to create membership interest.

Some people like to show evidence that "they belong" and "they've been there." A membership card, a lapel pin, or a sticker to go on the car window provides them the means. A certificate of accomplishment is shown with pride. My fisherman friend proudly shows the Angler's Award he received for the large fish he caught in Manitoba, Canada. He also received a pin which he wears on his fishing jacket. The province of Canada has gained an enthusiast who will return to the resort area.

How to Get People to Think Positively

Thinking negatively turns people off. It discourages them and kills their enthusiasm. A negative thinker expects failure, disappointment, and poor results. Consequently, he is unable to get things done and often does not even want to try. The depressing part of his viewpoint is that only the bad things are seen; that, plus his tendency to inflate the negative, makes a situation appear much worse than it really is.

Thinking positively inspires people, enabling them to be more efficient, produce more, and do better work. Thinking positively means believing that things can be done, that problems can be solved, and that there is more good than evil in today's world.

The secret of getting people to think positively is to convince them that such thinking is best for them. You can prove this by first pointing out that the negative thinker doesn't even try—he doesn't give himself a chance to succeed. The positive thinker gets more enjoyment and satisfaction from life simply because he gets involved with more things; he is more active and interested. Coupled with his optimism, things work out better for him and he accomplishes more.

Another way of proving the worth of the positive viewpoint is to recount from history the feats of men who wouldn't accept failure and carried on to give the world inventions such as the airplane, the electric light, and nuclear energy. These inventions came about because someone believed they were possible, worked hard and optimistically and proved they were right.

Edward J. Feeney, vice-president of systems performance at Emery Air Freight Corp. of Wilton, Connecticut, is a strong advocate of "accentuating the positive." He believes that praising a worker will not spoil him, and he looks for a little good in the worst worker and then praises him for it.

The theory of "positive reinforcement" was first proposed by Harvard psychologist B. F. Skinner to improve worker performance. Feeney started using it after finding that the alternative—punishment—wasn't getting results.

A good instructor stresses the positive in his teaching. He tells and shows his pupils how a job *should* be done, not how it *should not* be done. The correct way of performing a job is learned instead of the incorrect.

Positive thinking on the part of leaders toward their subordinates makes the subordinates feel good and want to do a better job. But it goes beyond that. The worker who views his job with a positive viewpoint *because his boss was sincere and saw the good in his performance*, will be more satisfied with his work and will actually *do a better job*.

How Attitude Determines Someone's Future

The people who hire individuals for business and industry place a lot of weight on a person's attitude when deciding whether to offer him a job. They know that someone's attitude may be more important than his ability or skill.

H. A. Thompson, Personnel Manager for a large chemical company in Delaware, says, "We always try to determine a job applicant's attitude before we hire him, both by checking his references and by studying him during an interview. Attitude is more important to us than experience, because if an applicant has the right attitude, he will learn and grow to compensate for any experience that he lacks. If we suspect or see a poor attitude, we will hesitate to hire."

The matter of attitude is often the deciding factor in today's industrial plants when a supervisor or foreman is to be chosen from among the workers. If you find yourself in a situation where you want to promote one of your people to a supervisory position, you would be wise to seriously consider the attitude of each promising individual. The man with the enthusiastic and positive viewpoint is much more likely to do a good job than the man who has pessimistic or negative inclinations.

A personnel man in a Midwest publishing house defended his decision to hire an individual for an assistant editor's position despite the applicant's lack of training in journalism by saying, "I like her attitude—she may go far with the company because of her strong empathy for people as well as being meticulous in what she does. Conscientious people are needed in our line of work."

9

How to Handle
the Problem Person

When machinery or equipment breaks down it can be repaired or replaced. When a plan or program fails to give desired results it can be changed. The solution isn't so simple when people fail to do their job or behave abnormally. Most leaders and managers have recognized that people are much more of a problem than the machines they operate or the plans they follow.

Young people on the job frequently demand more individualism, and some of them carry it to extremes, causing problems for supervisors and the company. Workers are better educated than they were in the past. Many people expect more out of a job than they are getting, and many are not concerned if they lose their jobs. These things coupled with rapid changes in our society create differences in values that cause conflict.

To some extent we're all problems to our bosses and to ourselves. Our difficulties on the job are caused by our emotions as much as by our lack of skills. The more we are able to conform and control what we do, the fewer problems we seem to have to face. Getting along with other people is more important than having a high degree of skill.

A problem person is a poor performer. He either does a poor job of his own or he interferes with other people trying to do theirs. In handling

the problem person, you need to bring his performance up to an acceptable level, see that he gets along with other people, and enable him to get
satisfaction from his work. Here are some suggestions on how you can
accomplish these objectives.

How to Deal with the Lazy Worker

An employee who is just plain lazy is a real problem to any
manager. He doesn't get the amount of work done that he should,
making himself and the department look bad. Jobs are delayed and costs
are higher because of him. Worse, his reluctance to do something
constructive may influence other borderline employees to also "dog" it
a bit. How should he be dealt with?

Saul W. Gellerman, President of Management Develop-
ment/Employee Relations of Gellerman-Kay Corporation, feels that
most people who don't like to work were not that way originally. They
have been turned off by "the establishment" and by working at levels
below their ability. Gellerman says that there are very few "bad apples"
in the working ranks, and that most cases of inefficiency and poor work
are the result of a weak organization or bad ways of doing things.

If you seem to have more than your share of reluctant workers you
might take a good look at how the jobs in your organization compare
with other jobs. If there were a job opening would you recommend that a
friend of yours apply for it? What do most of your people think of the
company? Maybe the job rather than the individual is at fault for poor
performance.

The lazy worker requires closer supervision than other workers do
if he's to be kept busy. His foreman can do this by frequently asking him
if he needs help when he is idle, or if he understands what he is to do.
Praise and thanks for what he accomplishes may overcome some of the
lack of satisfaction he apparently gets from working.

When Arthur LaBlanc, chief operator at the Norwich, Connecticut
Pollution Abatement Facility, finds he has a sluggish worker he talks to
him to find out why he is shirking his job and whether he's happy with
what he's doing. If the worker has no excuse and makes no attempt to
change his ways, LaBlanc gives him a warning. Frequently LaBlanc
will find that the individual who does not want to work has a personal

problem involving money or his family, and after he has talked about it, he'll get back on the job.

One approach that is often effective in getting more from the lazy worker is to team him with someone who is very conscientious. "Exposure" to the performance of such an individual may be influential in starting and keeping him moving, especially if the peer also does a bit of prodding. Social pressure brought by fellow workers is always harder to resist than what you as his superior could exert.

How to Cope with Lateness

While continually being late may be an outward sign of a lack of enthusiasm and interest for the job, it is often simply a poor habit which the individual has adopted in his life pattern. Some people are late everywhere they go. They are difficult to change.

One of the hardest types of late arrivers to handle is the individual who is regularly late but his lateness amounts to only a few minutes. His tardiness is not usually enough to affect other people's performance, but he still loses time on the job. Not knowing if he will arrive at all creates a further irritation among those who depend on him.

The best way to cope with such an individual is to talk with him after each offense. Ecnourage him to be on time and stress that you expect him to be. Point out that other people notice when he is late and may wonder if this laxness also carries over into his work. If they've once reached this conclusion, they may never feel otherwise.

Gene Sankey, section head in accounting at Goodyear Tire & Rubber Company, has one of his clerks take attendance in the department every morning soon after starting time. The record, which also accounts for individuals who are sick or on vacation, goes to the department manager. Anybody who is frequently late must give reasons for it to the manager.

The employee who periodically arrives much later than only a few minutes must be dealt with differently. Lateness of more than half an hour due to oversleeping, for example, is inexcusable if it occurs more than once—the individual deserves a reprimand.

William Barr, foreman with Bell Telephone Co. of Pennsylvania, New Castle District, docks a man's pay after a third lateness violation.

He also warns the man that docking will continue with further offenses and reminds him that lateness hurts his chances for promotion.

How to Help the Misfit

Much of today's productivity is the result of group efforts. People working in pairs or teams are a way of life in many industrial operations, especially in assembly-type work. The fellow who doesn't "fit" in this scheme is a problem to himself and his company.

How is this fellow different and why isn't he accepted as a member of the group? Knowing the job and being capable of doing it are not the reasons he is having trouble. He's different because of dress or education. He may be out of place because of his interests or the way he talks. Whatever, he sticks out like a sore thumb, and the people he is trying to work with may be rejecting him.

You have an obligation to help the misfit. Remember, he has as much right to his job as anybody else. If he does his job satisfactorily your task may be formidable.

The way to attack the problem is to sit down with the individual for a frank discussion of the situation. Indicate your willingness to help, but point out the difficulty in trying to get people to accept him if you order them to do so. Ask his opinion on whether he would consider another job in the company where he might not encounter the same situation.

You have the alternative. Getting the group on his present job to accept him requires that you do a good job of selling. Convince them that he has a right to hold the job the same as they do. Also, you may say that you are not asking for his acceptance *socially*, just acceptance on the job. Most people will go along with an appeal for justice. But occasionally the misfit has to make the greatest adjustment if he is to gain acceptance.

Ben Russo, utility worker in a metal fabrication plant, bitterly complained to his supervisor that he was being made the butt of practical jokes, some of which were destructive of his belongings. His tools were frequently coated with black grease as was the handle on his locker door. His work gloves were often cut or stolen. He never was able to catch his tormentors in these acts, and nobody ever knew who the guilty persons were.

Russo brought on much if not all of his harassment by his belligerent, taunting treatment of his fellow men. He was frequently heard publicly deriding one individual or insulting another. The solution to his problem seemed almost impossible since his loud complaining of his mistreatment to management and to anybody who would listen to him only served to "feed the fire" of his antagonizers.

Management's appeal to union representatives to pass the word to the guilty ones to stop such practices on the threat of punishment if caught did not bring a halt to the tricks. Only after Russo's supervisor had a frank discussion with him about his own behavior followed by a change on his part, was the frequency of the "grease treatment" and "lost gloves" reduced and eventually discontinued.

If your efforts fail to solve the problem of the misfit, you must insist on a change of jobs for him. Be sure that he understands why this must be done and that you hold nothing personally against him.

What to Do About Work Pace

In every organization there is usually at least one worker whose performance isn't up to the average. If he's working with other people on an assembly line or other group effort, he may hold back the output of the entire group. Obviously, something has to be done in the interest of efficiency.

Dr. Gavriel Salvendy of the State University of New York at Buffalo has studied this problem by measuring the work pace of individuals. He has concluded that no *average* work pace can be established for most humans. Salvendy feels that work pace is a part of a person's personality and is individual, like the shape of one's face.

His studies have shown that an individual is most efficient when he works at his own freely-chosen pace. If you push him too fast, his efficiency declines. Workers tend to speed up as they get older. When younger workers set their own pace, they work more efficiently, while older workers perform at about the same efficiency, regardless of who sets the pace. Older men work more continuously than younger men simply because they are older and trying to prove themselves.

If one of your people is not keeping up with his group you should try to change his job. He will probably do a more efficient job elsewhere

where the work pace better fits him. But first make sure he undersands the situation. Give him the opportunity, if he wants it, to try to improve. Point out that unless he changes, you will have to move him. Keep your word.

How to Handle the Talker

The individual who likes to talk may know how to do his work and even be proficient at it. The problem is that because of his yen for gabbing he doesn't spend enough time working. Worse, his continual talking and his reluctance to end a conversation may not only annoy his boss and his fellow workers, he keeps them from working, too.

Typically, the talker gives long answers to questions, constantly repeats himself, digresses from the subject, and likes to present the pros and cons of the solution of any problem.

How do you silence such an individual? Strategies vary; some work with good success. Ideally, keeping him busy so he doesn't have time to talk is the best approach from the viewpoint of getting things done, but some talkers aren't materially deterred by the press of work. If the individual does have assignments due, however, you can halt the flow of words with a simple question about the status of a job (pleading for a simple, short answer!).

Try having a frank talk with the individual about his problem; mention how you avoid excessive talking yourself to show him that other people also have the problem. This will tend to take away part of the guilt feeling he may have from your concern. A good point to make is that everyone on the job should be conscious of the value of time, and that too much talking takes up valuable time of both the talker and the listener.

Another way to contend with the talkative worker is to remove his listeners or make them inconvenient to him. Managers can easily bring about a separation with a few words such as, "That's all I have for now," or, "I'll talk to you later," followed by physically leaving him. Sometimes you may have the opportunity to lead away one of his listeners by requesting a private discussion with the listener on another matter. You might also consider relocating the talker's desk closer to files and away from other people's desks.

The manager of an accounting department of a large company in New York found that there was too much "visiting" by his people whose desks were along an aisle between other departments. People going from one department to another continually stopped to talk with these employees. His answer to the problem was to have a six foot high partition wall put on both sides of the aisle. To not make the partitions too unattractive, the upper portions were constructed of glass. Friendly greetings still are possible but long conversations have been eliminated.

A busy storeroom manager in an industrial equipment supply house has devised a way to break off visits with gabby salesmen without offending them. He prearranges to have one of his people call him on the phone after a few minutes requesting his immediate attention on a matter away from the office. The manager explains, quickly winds up the conversation, and leaves. So do the salesmen.

How to Give Criticism

In your working with people it is inevitable that you will encounter criticism. You may be criticized by your superiors, your peers, and even your subordinates. You will need to periodically criticize someone yourself. You should know how to go about it.

People are criticized for three reasons: to prevent similar mistakes in the future, to suggest different behavior, and to improve their efficiency.

You must follow some rules if you wish to do an effective job of criticizing. First, recognize that nobody enjoys being negatively criticized—it lowers their sense of importance and hurts their pride. Moreover, if it isn't handled properly, it can cause resentment and irritation. A skillful manager knows how to criticize someone without hurting him.

Getting all the facts is a major prerequisite. Since many of the facts you need are about the individual you are going to criticize, you must get them from him. The best way to do this is to simply ask him the question, "What happened?" If you ask for facts, *and listen,* rather than try to immediately place blame, you are more likely to get the information you need.

Giving criticism without causing harm requires tact and diplomacy. One of the tricks of the trade is not to criticize until you have first made some comment about achievement and usual good performance. This softens the blow and assures the recipient that you still regard him favorably.

The manner in which you criticize is a determinant of your effectiveness. Losing your temper, being sarcastic, and showing disgust are crude ways of handling it. Giving criticism need not be an emotional event. A calm, helping tone will get a better response.

Criticism should always be conducted in private to avoid personal embarrassment. Everyone has pride and there is no reason for you to unnecessarily attack it. The recipient of your criticism will be grateful for thoughtfulness on your part in this respect.

A number of college students were studied in a research effort to learn the effects of praise and blame on human performance. The students were divided into several groups and each group was given a series of mental tests requiring speed and accuracy. When the students had completed the first series, each group was told of their performance in a different way. One group was praised in front of the other groups; another was privately reprimanded; a third was reprimanded in front of the other groups; and so on. Then the groups were given further tests.

The results of the second tests showed the beneficial effects of private criticism in that it got better results than criticism given in public. Private reprimand produced almost twice as many cases of better results as public reprimand. More students who were criticized publicly turned in worse second performances than those who were criticized privately.

The main purpose of criticism is to suggest a better way of behavior. Since most people want to do well, you should try to help them do so. The way to provide that help is to suggest how it can be done. This is the positive approach and the only one that works.

Placing Blame

Everyone needs to periodically hear how he is doing, whether he is performing his job correctly, and if he is doing as much as is expected of him. People look to their leaders for this information. You can either give someone credit or blame. In all probability, most of your appraisal will be on the credit side, or the individual will not continue on the job.

Credit rewards someone in that it consists of praise and recognition. Blame criticizes someone by fixing the responsibility for an error or fault on an individual. Although opposites, both are motivators in that they usually cause a change in behavior.

Psychologically, people expect to be blamed when they have erred. Moreover, it may do them some good if it relieves their guilt feelings. However, blame should not be harsh. You should prefer to look for a technique to "save face" for your listener, to blame a failure on conditions for which he is not responsible. In this way he will not need to defend himself, to alibi, or to explain.

Every problem can be blamed on one of four conditions: people, materials or things, nature, or government. To save face for your listener, pick the condition he probably would. Minimize the harm, and look for some good or benefit in it. You can always say, "At least we found that won't work!"

Joseph Dodson, technical director at Jones Chemical, feels that he gets across the placing of blame for an error by one of his people by only recounting the thinking or series of events which led to the mishap. He is careful to say, "so it will not happen again" and avoids pointing the finger at any individual.

When placing blame, leave the guilty fellow corrected but not torn apart; allow him to retain his dignity.

How to Use Discipline

Managers have the responsibility for seeing that rules are enforced. If discipline is necessary, then managers must have the courage to see that it is administered. Weak organizations sometimes get that way because leaders allow subordinates to take advantage of them.

Some managers hesitate when it comes to trivial rules, and that attitude often causes problems, says Donald S. Baigent, chief industrial engineer, Smith-Victor Corp., Griffith, Indiana. He feels that all rules should be enforced because a rule that appears trivial in one area may be important in another. The leader who doesn't have the overall view may find a rule difficult to understand but this doesn't relieve him of the responsibility for enforcement.

Nobody likes to discipline someone. It's one of the unpleasant jobs that managers must perform, but much of the unpleasantness arises from a misconception of what discipline really is.

Disciplining is a *correcting* act, not a punishing one. When a manager disciplines an individual he should teach him rather than reprimand him. Disciplining should be a positive act such as guiding and training. Many leaders think of it as a negative act in that it involves "bawling out" or penalizing. Disciplining an individual is mainly the responsibility of his immediate supervisor who originally gave him his on-the-job training and saw that the company's policies and procedures were made clear. Rule-breaking is often the result of inadequate teaching; if this is the case, the teacher should be made aware of it.

You can avoid the problems of rule-breaking. By being alert and watching for laxity you can put a stop to forbidden practices early, before they become habits. Disciplining can be minimized if individuals are constantly evaluated for performance and behavior. When deviations appear, immediate action should be taken to correct or clear up misunderstandings. For example, the manager who permits tardiness or loafing to go on after a few incidents without talking to the offender is failing in his job.

Six Steps in Disciplining

The better you know an individual, the better job you can do of disciplining him. With one individual you may need to be firm, even demanding, since this is the only type of treatment that will get corrective action. The same type of treatment with another individual may be too drastic and cause hurt—here a mere suggestion of the need for change is sufficient.

When disciplining *is* necessary, plan to devote some time to it rather than trying to get the matter handled quickly. Here are some suggestions on how to proceed:

1. Try to do your discussing as soon as you can after the incident requiring it has happened. Both you and the individual will more easily remember the incident and the matter will not have been allowed to become worse.

2. Talk to the individual *in private*, away from where other people

can see or hear you. You do not want the individual to be embarrassed or "lose face" in front of his friends and peers.

3. Be friendly and informal in discussing the problem. Let the individual tell his side of the story first so that you can get the facts and details. *Listen* carefully to get his viewpoint and give him the benefit of any doubt.

4. Weigh and decide the facts before you constructively discipline. Avoid "harping" and "nagging" in your talking. Carrying on after you have made your point can only cause irritation.

5. Control your emotions and those of the individual, if possible, during the discussion. Arguing does not help. Try to have the individual see the seriousness of the problem and why he should change his attitude or performance.

6. Determine the reaction from your discipline. See if the individual feels he is being treated fairly and understands what you expect of him. Try to get a promise from him to do better in the future.

Bad feelings needn't be a result of disciplining someone if you handle it correctly and follow-up afterward. At your first opportunity be friendly and interested in how the individual is getting along. He'll realize that you don't carry a grudge and that his past discretion is not going to be held against him.

How to Treat Abnormal Behavior

Often you must work with someone who easily becomes angry, rude, mean, or overly emotional. Some people chronically behave this way; others do so only periodically.

The normally stable individual who temporarily displays extreme emotion may do so because of being overworked or tired. He could also be not feeling well or become irked with small irritations. His bad mood will soon pass so you should put off discussion with him if you can until he is back to normal.

What should you do if you happen to be present during a rare outburst? Keep your mouth shut—you have no right to intrude. If you feel out of place at the moment you might say, "I realize that you may wish to handle this matter first, so I'll return later." When you do return he will be very considerate because of your previous tact. But don't bring up the incident. He will mention it if he wishes to discuss it.

The fellow who frequently "flies off the handle" and is constantly upset is a tougher problem. Basically, he is emotionally immature. He has a poor personality and it is not likely to change. It does no good to postpone your business with him. He will probably be just as hard to talk to tomorrow as he is today.

In order to get along with him, you must stress how *he* will benefit from what you propose. *His* interest should come first if there is a choice in any matter. He may have a strong inferiority complex. Try to accept his viewpoint, and agree whenever you can. Listen to his gripes and sympathize with him. If you have some common interest, talk about it. You should have no hope of changing him, only of getting along with him.

You will always find it difficult to decide how to treat someone who behaves abnormally. Recognize what you are facing and make the best of it. Surprisingly, if you try to go along with someone with this weakness instead of fighting it, you may find that he soon treats you better than others and that you really don't have a tough problem after all.

Four Ways to Handle Personality Problems

People with personality problems are that way because of their strong emotions and their outlook on life. Such people may feel that they are being persecuted unfairly and that everybody is against them. Some may be over-aggressive or hostile, others are very submissive or dependent. How you handle such people determines if their personality quirks become major human relations problems. Here are some things to do and some not to do in working with them:

1. Avoid getting involved in emotional problems. Such matters should be left to psychiatrists and psychologists—you do not have the skills unless this is your field. Also, it is too easy to become trapped by your own feelings which then compound the problem.

Recommend professional help only if you can do so tactfully. The best person to suggest this should be the company doctor or a close friend.

2. Try to help the individual by teaming him with someone compatible. For example, put two aggressive people together rather than a meek individual with a bold one. One exception, however: coupling an apprehensive fellow with a confident, mature partner may help the fearful one.

3. Consider reassignment to put the problem employee more at ease. Some people must have clean surroundings, others cannot stand noise; one may be afraid of heights, another cannot stand the slightest confinement. Try to find tasks for people which do not bother them. Match people to the job. Their "problems" may be minimized or disappear if you do so.

If you are accused of playing favorites, explain your reason for what you are doing. Most people are fair if you explain problems of this sort to them.

4. Do a good job of persuading and selling the individual when he is unhappy with conditions. Many times the temporary aspects of a situation can be pointed out and will be accepted. Other times special provisions can minimize or alter a situation so that it is less objectionable.

Why People Lose Their Jobs

People seldom lose their jobs because they do not have the necessary job skills or do not know how to do their work. Dr. Kenneth McFarland, educational consultant of General Motors Company reports that "90 percent of dismissed employees fail because they do not get to work often enough, show up on time, or do enough after arriving. They *know* enough to hold their jobs but they cannot get along with other people."

People show their failure to get along with others in several ways. For example, they can be dishonest or disloyal; they can be stubborn and controlling; they can be egotistical and fail to give credit; they can be liars and hypocrites; they can fail to keep promises and be uncooperative. Make sure you're the opposite of all these if you want to hold your job and impress upon your people to do the same.

Of course, we can lose our jobs for reasons other than being unable to get along with other people. Nobody is perfect and even the best of us make mistakes. We know that "to err is human." But must we make mistakes simply because we are human? When it comes to personal matters, we usually don't make many mistakes. We watch how we spend our money, how we handle our property, and how we treat our family and friends. But some of us are not so careful to avoid job errors involving these same things. We're not always careful with the company's money, we mistreat its property, and we don't do a good job of getting along with customers or other employees.

The reason for our lack of care on the job is our failure to realize that job errors are just as personal and damaging as errors we commit off the job. If we are careless we can get in just as much trouble on the job as off it.

Firing the Poor Worker

Some manager's tasks are very distasteful. One of these is having to fire someone. If you have people working for you, some day you will probably have to do this job. How do you decide when this must be done? How do you go about it?

You must be sure that firing the individual is the only way the problem can be solved. Deciding this requires that you thoroughly study him. You would be justified in your decision if any or several of the following conditions exist:

1. The employee is a troublemaker and continually looks for ways to disrupt the organization and to lower the morale or negatively alter attitudes of other people.

2. Nobody is able to get along with the individual. Many quarrels and misunderstandings result from his actions or inactions.

3. The individual doesn't do his job because he refuses to apply himself. He is not interested in learning.

4. The employee causes his company to look bad to the public. His actions result in lost sales or poor public relations.

Before you fire anybody you should talk to him, pointing out why his performance is inadequate or unacceptable, and requesting that he change his ways. You should try to help the employee with his problem, listening to him and trying to understand why he acts as he does. You must be sure you do not fire someone because of bias or prejudice.

Perhaps training or guidance by other people would be of help. The personnel department of your company may want to advise you and also talk to the individual. If you meet with failure in such steps, you should follow up with at least two warnings that his job is in jeopardy unless he improves.

Hubert Hall, executive of an assembly line plant in Detroit, says, "I've never been accused of showing partiality or of being discriminatory. Everyone gets a fair shake from me and they know it. If I fire a man, he knows he deserves it. And the rest of my employees will back me up on it."

Robert Townsend's philosophy for handling a problem employee is worth noting. He feels that your first step should be to try to help the worker. But you can spend only so much time on that. "If you can't make a man into what you want him to be within two years, let him go. He's a human being in a situation where the chemistry is wrong. And he may be eaten up inside by something. If you can't figure out what it is and he can't tell you, it's much better for him to go. Maybe he's in the wrong industry. After you've satisfied yourself that you've tried, get rid of him."

If your conscience bothers you because of firing someone, remember that your other people deserve fair treatment and that firing a poor employee can't hurt them. In fact, they may question your management ability if you don't fire someone when the need is obvious.

How to Manage the Dead-ender

Every organization has people who have reached a job level where promotion is out of the question—they have reached a dead end. Moving them to a higher position would put them beyond their capabilities, risking both the individual's morale and self-esteem as well as the company's welfare due to incompetent performance. How do you manage such people to keep them motivated and happy with their work?

The president of Universal Foods Corp., Milwaukee, Robert T. Foote, believes that the best way to motivate persons for whom promotion is unlikely is to make their personal objectives and the company's objectives compatible. He suggests manager-subordinate talks as the vehicle for achieving this compatibility. The manager can explain what the company expects from the individual without setting unrealistic goals. He can make the individual feel that what he is doing is something the company needs.

Job enrichment is another way of keeping the dead-ender interested in his job and his company. Redesigning, expanding, and altering a job without going beyond the capabilities of the individual holding that job permits him to grow, develop, and most important, maintain his enthusiasm for the work.

Managers of people who occupy dead-end jobs must take the responsibility of keeping these people alert and contributing to their company. Managers can do this by delegating more of their own work. Subordinates, in turn, can grow by asking for more responsibilities from their superiors. If both of these actions are taken, the dead-ender may never really feel that he has truly reached the limit of his capabilities.

10

How to Get Jobs Done

Every organization wants and needs people who can get things done. An individual who has this capability is welcome and can hold a job with most any company. Of course, such a person cannot do it all by himself. If he is a manager, he knows how to motivate, persuade, and lead people in accomplishing objectives and reaching goals.

People who get jobs done have a philosophy and viewpoint which enables them to inspire others. They know how to approach them and they are aware of the roadblocks to progress that they must overcome in themselves and their subordinates in order to succeed.

If you have the strong desire to get things done, see problems solved, and experience the satisfaction coming from jobs well-handled, here are the ways to go about accomplishing these things.

How to Change a Poor Attitude About Work

If people are to get jobs done, they must be work-oriented, that is, have an attitude favorable towards work. In a recent study of the attitudes of working people, a large group was asked if they enjoyed their work. Many responded in the negative. Those that did explained that the word "work" adversely affected their emotions and self-discipline. Work to them meant a taking away of some of their individuality. They had to "give" something of themselves when they worked. They related it to not having a choice of what they would like to do to make something of themselves and "to contribute."

Since everyone wants to be someone important, the problem facing employers is how to enable their people to reach personal goals while achieving company goals. An attitude must be developed in the employee that work is a *positive* thing and that through it both the individual and the company can gain.

A manager who wants to change the poor attitude of a subordinate must find and promote a positive relationship between the subordinate and himself that is stronger than the negative one then existing. To do this, the manager needs to improve his communications so that more freedom to exchange thoughts exists and more mutual trust is developed.

Research by the U.S. Department of Labor shows that most people derive a great deal of satisfaction from their work, and believe that management has the right to determine company policy. Most workers don't want something for nothing.

A subordinate's poor attitude may have developed because he didn't have or receive facts which would have led him to continue to feel otherwise. Such information must now be provided. In addition, the necessity for a change in his attitude should be made clear to him and ways to bring it about suggested. His leader should explain how the change will benefit him such as result in easier working conditions, a better job, more pleasant relationships with peers and superiors, and even ease his troubled mind. The leader should give him a chance to see how a change in his attitude will also help other people.

Allowing the subordinate to plan his own change and bring it about in his own manner lowers his resistance to the change. Nobody should be made to feel that he is being "forced" to turn about, even though it may basically amount to that. The "or else" tag attached to a pill makes it more difficult to swallow.

Unfortunately, some people with poor attitudes do not want to help themselves. If you run into this, the best you can do is offer understanding and a willingness to help. Such people must see this weakness in themselves before they will change.

How to Get Willingness on the Job

Many people resist authority, and very few people like to take orders. Most workers resent being "told" to do something. Well then, how should you approach someone to do a job for you?

The right way is to "ask" someone to do a job, not "tell" him. A smart leader says something like this: "Would you please answer the phone for me today, Mary? Betty is sick and won't be in."

This approach has three things going for it. You requested a job, not demanded it. You explained why you asked for the help. And you used the individual's name which added a personal touch.

Enthusiasm and a good attitude help to get jobs done. You can promote these by the way you give someone an assignment. Show that you have confidence that the individual will find the job within his capability and also that he will get some satisfaction from it. Play up the reason for it and its importance.

Bob Perkins, lab manager for a large company, had a problem —his technicians didn't seem to be very interested in their work. He solved the problem when he learned that they liked their work better, and thereby accomplished more, when he took the time to give them background information on the studies he was asking them to do. For example, he would tell a chemist who was testing a new compound what the compound should contribute to the formulation and why it was being tested. Explaining the theory along with what the lab was looking for in a new compound raised interest and curiosity. Some of Perkins' people now are anxious to complete their tests to see if the new material will produce a better product.

You may need to be a good salesman when you ask for a difficult or unusual job to be done. Be sure to do enough explaining. You can also help by demonstrating.

Ted Hager, a line foreman with Wallaceburg Hydro, Wallaceburg, Ontario, Canada, attests to the value of demonstrating. He says, "If I *tell* a man something, he'll forget part of it. So I *show* him, and the more I show him, the more he'll remember."

Think back. Weren't you more willing to try something new after someone demonstrated *how* it was done than right after you were merely *asked* to do it?

How to Manage by Objectives

A generally accepted mark of an efficient manager is a high skill in setting and achieving objectives for his people. Management by objectives is not a revolutionary method of managing, but simply a currently accepted procedure for carrying out the functions of management under a definite plan. It achieves this end by setting job responsibilities and performance standards for each member of a group. Although each member has his own objectives, all members work toward a common goal. The manager directs and melds individual efforts into a team performance.

There is no question that subordinates will do a better job if they are aware of their responsibility and the level of performance expected of them. Moreover, the managerial functions are clearer and more easily administered if such responsibilities are understood by both the manager and the subordinates. The capabilities and potentials of individuals are utilized to a greater extent when responsibilities and objectives are clearly defined. In simple words, more things get done.

How a Job Is Analyzed for Responsibility

It comes as a surprise to many managers to learn what subordinates believe are their responsibilities. Individuals often have never been told completely what they are expected to do, or they may have forgotten some details in the confusion of getting started on the job. Although an important job responsibility of the manager is to make constructive criticism of his subordinate's performance, criticism for non-performance can never be justified unless clear understanding has been reached of job responsibilities earlier.

The problem is best attacked by having the manager and the subordinate make separate lists of what each believes are the subordinate's job responsibilities. When the lists are compared, agreement should be reached on those items which will be adopted. Such agreement works for the betterment of both parties since both then know what is expected of the subordinate.

Job descriptions are often too general to be relied upon for covering the entire responsibility of a position. Many write-ups of duties are antiquated and obsolete, if they exist at all. A department which adopts management by objective principles should review its job descriptions periodically and bring them up-to-date even though they are not complete in detail.

How Level of Performance Is Defined

A subordinate needs guidelines which will enable him to determine how well he is doing. He should know how competent he must be to meet the job responsibilities.

By setting standards for job performance, the manager acquaints himself with and also gives the subordinate a level by which to judge the quality and quantity of his work output. Such standards bear a level of authenticity which make them of value. They are preferable to judgments of "sufficiency" which may be oral and easily forgotten.

The use of standards enables an individual to aim at self-improvement and to judge where in his performance he needs to put forth more effort. Through standards he can also recognize if a change in viewpoint is needed, gauge his growth, and determine his overall performance.

A level of performance for an engineer would define the depth and extensiveness expected of him concerning his engineering functions. With how much detail should he be concerned? How close should his relations be with other departments? How thorough should his reports be? These questions should be answered.

How Goals for Improvement Are Set

After responsibilities and levels of performance are defined, goals of achievement can be set for the subordinate to attain. These goals should, of course, be agreed to by both the subordinate and the manager. At this point, planning becomes a factor.

Planning is important since it incorporates the element of time in the development of the subordinate. Present ability and potential must be considered when setting objectives because a satisfactory level of performance may not be readily attainable if objectives are set too high. Then again, perfect compliance is not always necessary nor expected with subordinates. They need time to develop, gain experience, and demonstrate competence to themselves and others.

Often a manager should be content to limit a particular subordinate's goals in order to assure that he can make a good showing within a certain period of time. Discouragement through failure can thus be minimized or avoided. Such an approach also tends to build confidence and gain satisfaction, both of which aid in future endeavors. New objectives can always be set. The likelihood of reaching them is enhanced when past performances have been very good.

In discussing objectives with a subordinate, managers should be concerned more with *what* the subordinate's goals are than with *how* he expects to achieve them. Along the same line, the manager wants to see results rather than efforts without results.

As in all goal directed efforts, the follow-up by the manager plays an important part in evaluating achievements and accomplishments. Follow-up in the form of assessment also serves to help in the setting of future goals and levels of performance.

How to Handle Appraisals

One of the toughest jobs a manager has to handle is the appraisal interview with one of his subordinates. Yet this should be done on a regular basis. Many managers find that they are unable to communicate the need for improvement to some of their people. In addition, managers often have a problem with motivating their people. Perhaps the manager forgets that his own future depends on how well he prepares someone to take his place. Taking this into consideration could spur greater effort on the manager's part.

The appraisal should cover the objectives and goals previously agreed to by the manager and his subordinate. In the case of a staff engineer, his responsibilities might serve as the ground for the discussion, although they need not necessarily be mentioned item for item.

Thus, appraisals can consist of measurements which are meaningful since they can deal with specific items rather than generalities.

The performance appraisal is not intended to be a discussion of one's beliefs, personalities, or inclinations except as these are related to performance. What is of importance is how an individual applied himself and the degree of attainment realized from his efforts. Good work should be brought to light as it resulted in achieving goals, and inadequacies or weaknesses should be recognized as the cause for being unproductive.

All appraisal talks need to include plans for future performance. Agreements should be reached on unsatisfied goals and on new objectives. Decisions should be made on when programs should be started and when results should be expected. Everyone wishes to progress by improving his performance and justifying higher earnings. A manager helps a subordinate in this desire by his appraisal of him.

Management by objectives is basically concerned with achievement. Of secondary importance is competence, ability, experience, and motivation. This is not to say that these personal characteristics do not help an individual to reach his goals; but, if he does not reach them, it is of little concern of how hard he tried, or of the skills he had available to him. Similarly, a cooperative trait is desirable in a subordinate, but of minor significance if it does not lead to accomplishment. Management by objectives has been proven to be a good way to get jobs done.

How to Time Your Approach to People

It's to your advantage to learn as much as you can about the moods and temperaments of the people with whom you work. Knowing their "high" and "low" periods, when they are likely to be receptive, and when they are likely to be critical helps you in getting cooperation and in seeing that work is done.

Ralph Janson, staff manager at Acme Industries in Joliet, Illinois, learned from experience that the best time to go to the general manager on projects requiring his approval was late in the day. Morning meetings with him invariably encountered opposition, delays, and requests for further review.

Betty Freed, in her job of Research Director at Biological

Laboratories in Kansas City, knows not to push for reports on studies from technicians early in the week, especially not on Monday. She has found that her people's enthusiasm and drive on the job is enhanced if new projects are undertaken on that day. Winding up projects and preparing status reports are procedures which the technicians do better later in the week after they've "got in the swing" of things.

We see things differently from time to time, depending on our physical and mental condition. Whether we are relaxed or tired, and whether our body needs, such as hunger and sleep, are satisfied determines how we look at things at any particular moment. When we are angry or upset we find it difficult to think, to listen, and to perform to the best of our abilities.

You probably know someone who "doesn't want to talk" in the morning until he's had his cup of coffee or maybe a cigarette. Unless what you have to discuss with him is very urgent, you'll hit it off better if you wait until after he's had these "waker-uppers."

By recognizing that someone's feelings, mental or physical condition greatly affect how he acts, you can take advantage of timing. Consider this the next time you are about to suggest an idea or proposal to someone. Is it the right time? Would tomorrow or next week be better?

How to Cope with Procrastination

When assigning someone a job to be done, and you know your timing is right, it's good psychology to appeal to his reason that "now is the time." Use the importance to the overall goal of the organization and the challenge of the job as reasons for immediate attention. Urging quick action has another plus for it in that it tends to overcome procrastination.

The enemy of accomplishment is procrastination. At one time or another, you, along with many others, have been guilty of it to some degree. Procrastination is simply putting off doing something.

You procrastinate most often when you have an unpleasant task to do or when you must make a difficult decision. Your situation may be even more uncomfortable if you are not convinced that the task really needs to be done. A good example is the proposed washing of the kitchen walls which look fairly clean to you but dirty to your spouse.

While you are aware that you cannot continue to put off a job indefinitely, getting started on it is no easy matter. Best bet is to go after the job when you are fresh and in a good frame of mind. Once you start, keep at it until you finish. This saves facing the unpleasant thing a second time.

Not all of the elements related to procrastination are distasteful. When you finally finish a job which you have been putting off for a long time you'll get a bit more pleasure than you do from getting other jobs done—maybe a better word than pleasure would be "relief." At any rate, it's your reward for overcoming procrastination.

How to Make Your Job Easier

How much of the work that you do could be done by your subordinates? Do you frequently find yourself overloaded with detail work? Maybe you haven't yet adopted one of the key skills of managing: *the art of delegating*.

In case you're not sure about your need to delegate, let's look at some situations to help you decide.

1. Are you taking work home with you at night? Are you frequently working overtime?

2. Are those important jobs you're asked to do getting done just on time or a day or two late?

3. Are you unable to give the important jobs the amount of time they deserve? Is too much of your time being spent on the relatively unimportant jobs?

4. Are many of the things you're doing becoming routine in nature?

If you find that your answer to most of these questions is "Yes," then you should be thinking about delegating more of your work. This is particularly important if you have hopes of moving up in your organization. Your skill in delegating could be the deciding factor in whether you can handle greater responsibilities and a better job. A *successful* leader gets things done through others.

How to Overcome the Fear of Delegating

Many people say they believe in delegation yet neglect to practice it. *Why don't they?* They claim it is because they don't want to share their authority, because they are afraid of a subordinate moving up too fast, or because they feel they must do a job themselves to have it done right.

They're wrong on all counts!

The manager still has the authority after delegating; it's just a bit more indirect. A subordinate moving up fast shows your boss and others that you're ready for advancement; you've got a man about ready to take your place. You may feel that your subordinate cannot do a job as well as you can; is it really necessary that the job be done that well?

Unwillingness to delegate may also be a psychological problem involving fear. Examples of such fears are:

1. That credit for the job being done will go to someone else.

2. That it will become known that others know more about a particular job than you.

3. That someone may do the job better than you've been doing.

After you begin to delegate, these fears will become inconsequential or disappear entirely. You have much more to gain than to lose by delegating.

Six Steps for Effective Delegating

Effective delegating requires planning and thought, afterwards by action and follow-up. Let's look at the steps you should take to make it successful:

1. *See* the purpose of delegation. You have three basic objectives: to get the job done, to free yourself for other work, and to have your subordinate benefit by learning and experience.

2. *Decide* what you can delegate. Every person does some jobs which could be given to others. The amount and extent should be determined by how good a control you can maintain. In general, you should delegate as much of your work as possible. Do yourself only what no one else can do for you.

3. *Recognize* that subordinates will make mistakes; be willing to take the blame for those mistakes. Many mistakes can be avoided by making sure the subordinate understands what he is to do.

4. *Clarify* what you are delegating. Agree with your subordinate on goals and the limits of action which will be taken to reach them. Your subordinate must also understand what decisions are his and what decisions remain yours. Further, let others know of such arrangements so that he'll get the cooperation he needs to get the job done. Be sure that you and he follow the normal chain of command up and down in your communications on the job.

5. *Give* authority along with responsibility. Authority means making decisions and giving orders. An individual cannot be responsible unless he also has equivalent authority. Putting it in writing avoids misunderstandings and improves control.

6. *Follow-up*. Remember that you still have the final responsibility. But use it with diplomacy and tact. Best way is to ask your subordinates for progress reports and to set times for discussion of problems.

The art of delegating is not an easy task. You must *have* and *show* confidence in those to whom you delegate. That confidence will be motivation for them to perform to their best ability. It will also free your mind of worry and anxiety about the job being done properly and on time. Through your subordinate's performance, you will be able to extend yourself and your department.

How to Know If You Are Understood

Asking someone to do something for you does not guarantee that it will be done even though your listener may have been perfectly willing when you spoke to him. He may have interpreted your words as a comment, not a request. Or he may do something other than what you asked because he misunderstood.

Let's say, for instance, that you wish to get a safety message across to one of your people. You want to be sure he knows how to do his job the safe way. After you've talked to him and explained the safe procedure, you'd like to know if he understood. How do you find out?

What you need is feedback, a response that confirms that your message got through. If he asks questions, particularly if they are the type where he repeats your instructions in his words, you probably have been successful. You may need to ask the questions. Then the answers he gives will tell you if he understood.

At one of the Goodyear Tire and Rubber Company plants in Akron, the supervisional group use what they call Safety Feedback to determine if the workers know safe work procedures. Paul Tobey, Maintenance Supervisor, uses a group of general questions about the plant and the process that he asks a craftsman after he has become familiar with the plant, his job, and has read the Safe Practice Manual. If the craftsman can't answer the questions, Paul knows that he needs more training on safety and how to do his work.

How to Discuss Job Performance

A leader needs to periodically discuss with his people how they are doing with their work. If your subordinate is doing a good job, he deserves to be told so. Furthermore, if you don't tell him when his performance is unsatisfactory, how will he know that you expect him to do better? A performance review helps both the employee and the manager in their productivity and their working together toward goals.

Surveys have revealed that most employees want to know how they are doing and how they can improve themselves. Unfortunately, many managers are reluctant to discuss these things with their people. They worry that they may be wrong in what they tell an employee. They also want to be liked and respected; they fear that performance discussions will destroy these things.

Dr. William B. Plasse, a Whittier, California industrial psychologist, thinks the performance review can markedly improve employee development. He suggests four ways to conduct them to get the most benefit while retaining pleasant and comfortable relationships:

1. Be informal in choosing the time and place for a discussion, but be businesslike enough so that comments and suggestions will be taken seriously.

2. Ask for criticism of your own performance. Be sincere in wanting to hear if *you* are doing something wrong.

3. Keep records of general performance so that you don't evaluate by memory. Hold performance discussions at times other than when pay increases are due.

4. Conduct a broad range discussion in which responsibilities, potentials, training, and challenges are reviewed. Identify the strong and the weak inclinations of the employee in these areas.

Discussing job performance can eliminate any doubt an employee may have that his boss is not interested in him or his work. Also, through such discussions a leader has an opportunity to try to raise enthusiasm for the job in individuals who lack it.

Overcoming the Absentee Problem

Nobody today is self-sufficient. We all depend on other people. So when someone stays away from his job, his absence affects everyone. You have probably noticed what happens in your department when someone takes time off. It is no different when you are absent.

When you are not on your job either one of two things happens —your work doesn't get done, or someone else is asked to do it, either overworking him or sacrificing his work. If a substitute does your work it probably will not be done as well because he isn't as familiar with it.

Absenteeism hurts because it costs money, for the quantity and quality of work done is poorer. Too many people overlook this when they decide to take an unplanned day off.

Everyone should earnestly try to be on the job every day. The individual with a good attendance record is appreciated. Explain to your people why you need them on the job every day. And set an example for them by having a good record yourself.

How Being a Positive Thinker Gets Results

To get things done you must have a positive viewpoint. This means looking for reasons to do something rather than trying to find reasons why something can't or shouldn't be done. Resisting change is a negative position to take since change is inevitable if progress is to be made.

Getting things done should not be concerned with finding fault or placing blame. Too many times, time and effort is wasted in looking for someone to blame when an error is made or a problem not solved. The time could be spent better on the questions of what, how, when, why, and where in order to go forward.

A leader becomes discouraged when he finds his people believing that what they are doing is not constructive to progress, because when someone does not feel his work is worthwhile, he does not do his best. He also fails to put creativity or imagination into his efforts; his movements become mechanical rather than mental; his quantity of work may be satisfactory but his quality is poor.

The leader who comes across positively with his people combats the "it doesn't matter" attitude. You should try not to let such an attitude grow or prevail by keeping your people aware of the worth of what they are doing.

Be positive and enthusiastic. It helps to get things done.

How "Being Interested" Moves People Along

Do you show an interest in other people and their problems, or are you a "loner"? If you talk only about yourself people will soon tire of being with you. The man who shows concern with the problems of other men is better liked than the man who is indifferent or thinks only about himself. You can become more accepted in a month by showing interest in people than you can in a year by trying to get people interested in you.

Employees can and do get more done when they know their bosses are interested, especially when the bosses make themselves available for help on problems. A leader who shows he has control of a situation demands the respect and admiration of his people, and with those feelings comes the "pitching in" that gets jobs done.

How about your poise and calmness? Your ability to handle your job may be judged from your reactions when the going gets rough. The fellow who keeps his "cool" and an open mind is more receptive to others. He also gets jobs done.

Note how the successful personnel man is adept and remains in control when faced with a grievance brought in by an angry union representative. Yet, in another situation he gives the impression of being willing to go out of his way and demonstrates it by helping a disturbed employee with a personal problem.

Organizations need leaders who can "take charge." Only people who *are interested* have the motivation and capability to do an efficient job with other people.

Seven Ways to Keep the Wheels Turning

A manager can be a great influence on the initiative and drive of his people. He needs to be enthusiastic and continually looking for ways to maintain morale, build confidence, and motivate. His success in these efforts usually determines how much gets done and whether progress is being made. How does he accomplish these things? What can you do to get your people to produce and continue producing? Try these seven ways to keep those wheels turning:

1. Be a good listener when someone has a problem and wants to talk about it. Sometimes all someone needs is to get something off his chest and he'll get back to work. Regardless, talking about the problem expands communication so that understanding is improved.

2. Do a good job of planning and scheduling. Always know what comes next and how it should be done. Most importantly, let your people know these things. When subordinates understand their part in a transition or change-over period, they will not be confused or disturbed.

3. Keep people busy. Have assignments ready. Motivational experts say that a good way to get efficient work from employees is to

line up jobs for them to do and set times for when they should be completed. The worker who knows what job he's going to work on next day and what's expected of him feels that he is important and doing his share.

4. Try to solve "people" problems promptly. Letting them go invariably causes them to be exaggerated and hurts to become worse. Neglect and indifference suggest you don't care. Trouble prevented or caught early is much easier to contend with. Make yourself available to discuss complaints at the earliest opportunity and avoid trying to rush through them. Allow yourself plenty of time and give the other fellow your full attention.

5. Give people a chance to do their work without "bugging" them. Richard Waller, foreman at Bersted's Hobby-Craft Inc., Monmouth, Illinois, says that people work better if you "leave 'em alone and let them do their jobs." He points out that workers dislike to have a boss "looking for something wrong" and "pushing" for greater output.

6. Show your human side. You can demonstrate that you care about someone by visiting him when he's sick and remembering "special" days such as anniversaries. Learn to relax a bit on the job instead of always being serious. If you can "take the pressure off" your people periodically, they're more likely to come up with "second efforts" to solve problems.

7. Keep harmony by being fair. Avoid risking the loss of general cooperation by favoring a few. Praise when it's appropriate and criticize when it's deserved. It's not really how concerned you are about your people that keeps them on their toes, but it's how concerned they *think* you are.

How to Deal with Socializing

Should leaders socialize with subordinates away from the job? While the road to success in management-labor compatibility may be the maintaining of good relations, if your social life contains the same people as your business life, you may have trouble ahead. The difficulty is that such relations often cause on-the-job problems.

Personnel experts recommend that managers carefully limit their social relationships with employees outside the office because such mixing adversely affects objectivity. For one thing, discipline on the job becomes difficult to administer.

Another objection to social relationships with your people is that they weaken leadership in that chain of command tends to be ignored if employees from several business levels belong to the same social group.

Socializing on the job by managers is occasionally acceptable as a means of learning the other fellow's problems and "getting along" with each other because of mutual interests. Office parties, for example, are "musts"—up to a point, according to Chester Burger, president, Chester Burger & Co. Inc., New York-based management consultant. "If the boss doesn't participate, he's regarded as rude. He has to have the good sense to come in, be friendly, have a drink, and leave. If he becomes overly friendly, he's going to have problems. He should use his good judgment and discretion." The executive who lets down his hair at an office party on Friday "may be willing to be tough on Monday but his subordinates won't expect it."

How close, human to human, should you be with your people? Close enough to know their family, their hobbies, and their interests, but not close enough to drink and gamble with or borrow money from them, say management experts.

P.D.G.